Cook & Tell

Cook & Tell

No-Fuss Recipes and Gourmet Surprises

Karyl Bannister

Houghton Mifflin Company

Boston   New York

2001

For information about permission to reproduce selections
from this book, write to Permissions, Houghton Mifflin Company,
215 Park Avenue South, New York, New York 10003.

Visit our Web site: www.houghtonmifflinbooks.com.

Library of Congress Cataloging-in-Publication Data
Bannister, Karyl.
Cook & tell : no-fuss recipes and gourmet surprises / Karyl Bannister.
p.   cm.
Includes index.
ISBN 0-618-12761-5
1. Quick and easy cookery. I. Title.
TX833.5 .B36 2001
641.5'55 — dc21   00-054684

Codfish Cakes (page 178) is adapted from Point Club Fish Cakes, which
appeared in *Seafood Secrets Cookbook* edited by Ainslie Turner © Mystic Seaport,
Mystic, Connecticut. Melon with Prawns (page 81) originally appeared in
A Sussex Cook's Calendar by Prunella Kilbane, published by S.B. Publications,
1995. It is reprinted with permission of the author. Braised Celery and Carrot
(page 210) was adapted from Braised Celery, in *Real Irish Cooking* by Mary
Caherty, published by Robert Hale Limited, London. It is reprinted
with permission of the publisher. Sticky Gingerbread (page 326) originally
appeared as Hurry-Up Gingerbread, published in the booklet
*Old-Fashioned American Recipes for Cookies, Bread and Cake from
Mrs. Small's Kitchen and Conkey's Tavern* at The American Museum,
Claverton Manor, Bath, Avon. It is reprinted with permission of the publisher.

Designed by Melissa Lotfy
Cover illustration by Heidi Younger
Interior illustrations by Karyl Bannister

Printed in the United States of America

RRD 10 9 8 7 6 5 4 3 2 1

# Contents

To my husband, Bob,
who thinks everything I cook is wonderful,
so who am I to argue

Acknowledgments

I *have my father to thank for a love of* words and a respect for Liederkranz cheese. My mother kept me humble by mocking any reference I ever made to my fans, while I was writing what purported to be a food column for our local paper. "Your fans?" she would bellow, as if they mattered.

My mother-in-law, Barbara Webster Shenton, knew they did and actually wrote me fan letters. My father-in-law, Edward Shenton, came up with the title for the column and my newsletter, *Cook & Tell*. It has certainly come in handy, and I am grateful.

My daughter Amie gets a lifetime of hugs for apparently listening, or at least not interrupting, all those times I pushed her around as an infant in a supermarket shopping cart and needed to talk. She taught me it was OK to chatter away and never shut up when the subject was salad greens or ground beef.

I'm indebted to all the pros who coaxed my manuscript into a book. My agent, Doe Coover, saw the promise of a book beyond the bones of the newsletter. Senior editor Rux Martin saw a place for *Cook & Tell* on the Houghton Mifflin list; my editor, Lori Galvin-Frost, masterfully pulled from a ton of words a pound of publishable prose; designer Melissa Lotfy made everything look yummy inside, and jacket designer Martha Kennedy and cover illustrator Heidi Younger brilliantly captured the essence of *Cook & Tell* for the jacket.

There would have been no book without the newsletter and no newsletter without subscribers. I owe them each a big *Thank You* for sharing their recipes, anecdotes, and precious memories, all of which have helped to make *Cook & Tell* what many readers have called their "favorite piece of mail" through the years.

# Introduction

*T*he seeds for my newsletter were planted a week before my wedding. It had dawned on my mother, although not on me, that I was embarking on a major enterprise with a serious deficiency. I had no three-by-five card file of recipes, not a single family favorite committed to memory, and not even a scintilla of interest in cooking. In a week I'd be married, I kept telling her, and cooked food would just happen.

My mother would not listen. She strapped me into an apron, shackled me to the kitchen counter, and put me through a crash course in casseroles. I came out the other side with a speaking acquaintance with baked beans, scalloped ham and potatoes, and chili con carne. I was good for a week, counting leftovers and one night out.

My mother's concerns nevertheless had an impact on me. I took the *Joy of Cooking* on my honeymoon and read it on the long drive from Massachusetts to Texas. That book had been a shower gift from my cousin. Looking back, I think my mother put her up to it.

Little did I know that, as the years passed, the necessity of feeding a family would force me to trade in my ten thumbs and zero imagination for the fairly competent hands of a cook. For inspiration, I also had a mother-in-law who could spend all afternoon making dinner, enjoying every minute of the process. I began to embrace cooking as a hobby and a craft, not just a survival skill. I gave dinner parties; I experimented. I was always on the lookout for great recipes.

I like to talk. I like to meet people, and I wanted to know what they were cooking, so I talked the publisher of the local weekly into giving me a food column that was part day-in-the life, part recipes. Soon after, I decided to cast a wider net— to find out what was cooking outside my neighborhood—to people like me, who enjoyed relaxed, foody conversation and ideas they could latch onto immediately, without being made to feel dysfunctional for not using cilantro. Thus, what began as a weekly column grew into the monthly newsletter *Cook & Tell*.

In the manner of a recipe swap, the

newsletter's subscribers provide recipes and tips, including the ones that have made their reputations as cooks. Subscribers include a soup maker who dispenses his homemade soups to neighborhood shut-ins, a pastor who bakes a supreme blueberry pie, a single mother who recounts shortcuts she's used in feeding five children, and a woman who thinks there can never be enough chocolate recipes. Subscribers also include chefs and short-order cooks, food writers and critics, one of whom reckoned that the newsletter "fills the gap between Grandma's baking and a two-week vacation at the Cordon Bleu."

In keeping with the definition of *receipt,* the old-fashioned word for *recipe,* I have been but one receiver in a chain of receivers. Like many of my readers, I have tweaked and tinkered with many of the recipes, but it is not my wish to take credit for them. For this book, I've collected subscribers' favorites, as well as my own. Some of the recipes represent the easygoing food that real people dig into on a daily basis and want to talk about, fiddle with, and make again and again. Others were clipped from the pages of newspapers or magazines by avid collector cooks, who added notes in the cramped margins about optional ingredients and alternative methods. From tomato soup to seafood chowder, meat loaf

to filets mignons, cheesy mashed potatoes to glazed carrots, oatmeal cookies to a never-fail chocolate cake, *Cook & Tell* has all the meal requirements covered—and more.

Since *Cook & Tell* understands the frequent need to feed in a hurry, I include the "Cook It Easy" chapter, which proudly presents quick-to-fix main dishes, sides, and desserts. "Best Wishes, Best Dishes" offers special holiday favorites. "Good to Go" fills the niche when you need portable edibles that move easily to the backyard or porch or into a cooler for a longer trip. I lobbied for printing the chocolate recipes in brown ink, but had to settle for a chapter devoted to chocolate: "Chocolate Chitchat."

I've also thrown into the recipe mix the newsletter contingent's opinions, suggestions, and tips: thread potatoes on a barbecue skewer when baking for a large group, use instant potato flakes to thicken "white" chowder, heat sauerkraut in apple juice for best flavor.

It's a long way from my mother's kitchen, where I learned that cooked food doesn't just happen. I'm glad she finally made me learn. She gave me the nudge I needed to discover what fun it is to cook. Through twenty years and two hundred issues of my newsletter, subscribers have helped me pass the nudge along.

— *Karyl Bannister*

## Chapter 1

Bisque ◈ Bouillon ◈ chowder ◈ Soup

Soulful Bowlfuls

Soup ◈ Bouillon ◈ Consommé ◈ STEW

STOCK ◈ STEW ◈ chowder

Consommé ◈ potage ◈ BROTH

Spooner
or
ladle

you
realize

it's
time

for
soup

Old English Summer Soup

Serves 4

Add sweet lettuce and delicately flavored cucumber to vichyssoise and you have a whole new soup. In my mind's eye, I see Shirley Gibbs's kitchen in Wiltshire, England, where her wonderful AGA range is on all year round. Shirley's soup is simmering, and even though it's July, we'll have it hot. She's English. I'm making tea, but we'll have it iced. I'm American.

1 head Boston or Bibb lettuce	4–5 scallions (white and light green parts), chopped
2–4 tablespoons (¼–½ stick) butter	3 cups homemade chicken stock or canned chicken broth
2 medium potatoes, peeled and diced	Salt and freshly ground black pepper
6 inches of an unpeeled English cucumber (one of those long, virtually seedless jobs that cost a lot), diced, or 1 small regular cucumber, peeled, seeded, and diced	Heavy cream or half-and-half Snipped fresh chives, for garnish

Shred the lettuce by rolling up the leaves like a cigar and slicing them ever so thinly, *then* chopping the slices. Melt 2 tablespoons butter in a large saucepan over medium heat and sauté the lettuce, potatoes, cucumber, and scallions for about 10 minutes, or until the potatoes are softened, adding more butter if necessary. Add the stock or broth and salt and pepper to taste and simmer for about 20 minutes, or until the vegetables are tender. Cool until lukewarm, then puree in batches in a blender or food processor. Reheat in the pan to serve hot, or chill in the fridge to serve cold. Decorate with a little swirl of cream or half-and-half and a sprinkle of snipped chives on each serving.

Chilled Tomato-Cucumber Soup

Serves 4

Ginny Maxfield uses *canned stewed tomatoes, the kind with the onions, celery, and peppers mixed in, to produce a cold soup that delivers all the advantages of gazpacho, but doesn't require a whole lot of chopping. This was one of the slightly-chic-but-homey recipes that made Ginny's restaurant, Maxfield's, over the bridge in Boothbay Harbor, Maine, so popular for so long.*

2 14.5-ounce cans stewed tomatoes with onions, celery, and peppers, with their juice
1 English cucumber, peeled and cubed
1 teaspoon dried basil
1 teaspoon dried thyme
1 teaspoon dried rosemary, crumbled

1 teaspoon dried dill weed
1 teaspoon dried sage
1 teaspoon salt
Dash of Worcestershire sauce
Few shakes of Tabasco sauce
Sour cream
Chopped fresh parsley or chives, for garnish

Pour one can of tomatoes into a blender jar and put half of the cucumber cubes on top. To keep the cucumber from turning into mush, blend just until the cubes drop down to the blades. Transfer the first batch to a large bowl and repeat with the remaining tomatoes and cucumber cubes.

Add the basil, thyme, rosemary, dill, sage, salt, Worcestershire, and Tabasco, and mix thoroughly. Cover and chill for about 2 hours. Divide the soup among individual bowls, top each serving with a dollop of sour cream and a sprinkle of chopped parsley or chives, and serve.

GOOD SOUP

Mariah's Zucchini Soup

When your summer vegetable garden *begins to stretch from Z to shining Z, knock off a few of those zucchini with this breeze of a soup from my favorite bookseller, Mariah Hughs. The potato is a dandy thickener.*

4 cups chopped zucchini (about 2 medium)
1 medium potato, peeled and diced
1 small onion, chopped
2 bacon slices, chopped
2 tablespoons chopped fresh parsley
2 teaspoons chopped fresh dill or basil
1 garlic clove, minced
2 cups homemade chicken stock or canned chicken broth
Salt and freshly ground black pepper
Grated Parmesan cheese or sour cream, for garnish

Put the zucchini, potato, onion, bacon, parsley, dill or basil, garlic, and stock or broth in a large saucepan and bring to a boil over high heat. Reduce the heat to medium-low and simmer until the vegetables are tender, about 15 minutes. Cool until lukewarm. Puree in batches in a blender or food processor and add salt and pepper to taste. Serve hot or at room temperature, garnished with the grated Parmesan or sour cream.

Hey diddle diddle
The 🐱 and the 🎻
The 🐄 jumped over the 🌙

*I*nvite a group of friends who are good at milling about, sitting on the floor, and juggling bowls. Make three or four kettles of soup, all different, and a couple of special breads—maybe a big pan of corn bread and a few yeasty whole-grain loaves. If you wish, make the soups well in advance and freeze or refrigerate them; the wait is good for the flavors. If it's cold enough outside, set the kettles on the back porch until it's time to heat them up. Be sure there's a good lash-up between cover and kettle, unless you intend to invite the local raccoons.

So, the soup's on and the bowls are stacked up on the counter near the stove. The group gathers in the kitchen and hovers and sniffs and stirs and dips. After a bowl of Lentil Barley Soup, they return for Sweet-and-Sour Cabbage Soup, and later help themselves to Tomato Fish Chowder. Remember: Soup is compassionate. You can always add another cup of water or milk or a can of tomatoes and another bouillon cube and feed another mouth, if need be.

This kind of event invariably nets you a tidy legacy of leftovers. At least a couple of additional meals are assured, and the rest can be returned to a frozen state for a while.

The little 🐕 laughed to see such sport
and the 🥣 ran away with the 🥄

Magic Mountain Soup

Serves 12

Whenever my friend *Eleanor's family gathered at the cabin for a weekend of skiing, a chorus of voices would ask: "Who's going to make the Magic Mountain Soup this time?" And then somebody would volunteer to stay in and play chef. After five minutes of chopping, the ski-slope soup would be on the stove to simmer (say that five times, fast) until supper. Then there'd be all afternoon to stack wood and read that novel.*

No gourmet tour de force, this one's a kettle of honest-to-goodness soup that tastes just like meat and vegetables, because that's what's in it.

1 pound ground beef
1 1-pound bag frozen mixed vegetables (the conventional kind: peas, carrots, corn, string beans)
1 28-ounce can whole or crushed tomatoes, with their juice
3 carrots, peeled and chopped

3 celery ribs, chopped
1 onion, chopped
3 beef bouillon cubes
2 teaspoons chili powder, plus more if needed
1 teaspoon salt, plus more if needed
   Balsamic vinegar and grated Parmesan cheese, for garnish

Dump everything except the balsamic vinegar and Parmesan cheese into a kettle, pot, Dutch oven, or cauldron, whatever's at hand. Don't even brown the ground beef. Pour in water to cover by an inch or so. Bring to a boil over high heat, then reduce the heat to low and simmer gently, covered, for 2 to 3 hours. Adjust the seasonings and keep it bubbling until you're ready to ladle it out. Add a few drops of vinegar and a sprinkling of Parmesan cheese to each bowlful when serving.

Stock vs. Broth

Sara Gabrels, mildly frantic, is on the phone. "I'm making a chicken casserole. I have an inane question. It calls for chicken stock. I have broth. Is it going to work?"

"Darn right," I reply. "Here's what I think. Stock is what you make yourself out of real chicken, beef, or vegetables. Broth comes out of a can. Stock has the better pedigree, so it's probably 'best.' Use broth, use stock, use bouillon cubes and water. Use whatever you have. Go for it."

Golden Carrot Soup

Serves 14

For years, the ladies of Jo Ann Collins's church in Kenilworth, *Illinois, have been making huge quantities of her sunshiny carrot soup for their annual Holiday Luncheon Bazaar. The holiday they so tastefully celebrate is Christmas, but we proclaim Easter—or any other day of the year—a perfect time to indulge in such scrumptious bunny food.*

8 tablespoons (1 stick) butter

25 medium carrots, peeled and cut into ¼-inch-thick slices (about 10 cups)

2 large red bell peppers, sliced (about 4 cups)

3 medium onions, sliced (about 3 cups)

6 cups homemade chicken stock or canned chicken broth

1 cup fresh orange juice (from 3 oranges)

2 teaspoons grated fresh orange zest

1½ cups heavy cream or milk

Salt and freshly ground white pepper

Sweet rice vinegar

Chopped fresh parsley, for garnish

Melt the butter in a Dutch oven or other large, heavy-bottomed pot over medium heat. Add the carrots, peppers, and onions and stir to coat with the butter. Cook, covered, stirring occasionally, until the vegetables soften, about 8 minutes. Add the stock or broth and orange juice and bring to a boil. Reduce the heat to low and simmer, covered, until the vegetables are very tender, 20 to 30 minutes. Cool to lukewarm.

Puree the solids in batches in a blender or food processor until very smooth. (Quit now and freeze the puree to finish the soup later, or continue.) Return the puree, along with the liquids, to the pan. Add the orange zest, cream or milk, and salt, pepper, and vinegar to taste. Reheat, but do not boil. Garnish with the chopped parsley and serve.

 **Note**

* *This recipe makes a ton. If you freeze the puree in smaller quantities, you can add the cream and flavorings in proportionate dosages. Or halve the recipe and miss the fun of a whole lot of slicing.*

* *The church ladies spike their soup with Grand Marnier.* Cook & Tell *sends in sweet rice vinegar to add a flavor highlight. Marukan Seasoned Gourmet Vinegar is the brand I like. Many markets and fancy food stores, as well as Asian markets, stock it.*

County Clare Vegetable Soup

Serves 6

Jane Jentsch got this *from Mary Nolan, chef at the Clare Inn in County Clare, Ireland. It's the most user-friendly soup to come my way in a long time. Later, I learned that an Irish / British pint is twenty ounces, in comparison to our sixteen ounces. But there's nothing wrong with the results using the American pint measure. My way is thicker, plus you get more hunks of veggies per cubic inch of soup.*

> "I know, I know, big deal, vegetable soup. But take my word, it's cheap and it's great."
>
> — Jane Jentsch

4 tablespoons (½ stick) butter
2 large onions, chopped
3 celery ribs, chopped
2 large carrots, peeled and chopped
½ cup all-purpose flour

4 cups homemade chicken stock or canned chicken broth
   Salt and freshly ground black pepper
2 cups milk
   Chopped fresh parsley, for garnish

C hop the vegetables and fry them off in the butter," is Mary Nolan's way of saying melt the butter in a Dutch oven or other large, heavy-bottomed pot over medium heat. Add the onions, celery, and carrots and sauté until softened but not browned, about 6 to 8 minutes. Stir in the flour and cook for 2 minutes. Gradually add the stock or broth, stirring as the soup thickens. Bring to a boil, lower the

heat to low, and simmer, partly covered, for 15 to 20 minutes, or until the vegetables are tender.

Add salt and pepper to taste. Stir in the milk and heat barely to boiling. Garnish with the chopped parsley and serve hot.

Secret Soup Ingredients

According to Gene Simmons, "Soup is always better with parsnips added." If you're afraid someone's going to keel over if he finds out you're putting them in, add them on the sly, she counsels. "Put the peeled parsnips into the stock, take them out when they're done, mash them, and then put them back in for thickening."

Joan Wetmore says if you don't feel like parsnips, try turnips. "I make soup quite often, and I like the turnip flavor but not *pieces* of turnip." So she cooks a batch of turnips—"always add some sugar," she advises—and then mashes them and packs them into small plastic bags for the freezer. "Then I get one out for a pot of vegetable beef or bean soup. It gives excellent, but not strong, flavor. People don't even know what it is."

One-of-Each Soup

Serves 4

This is one wonderful surprise, *from herb lady Marion Bates. Every time I look at the recipe, I don't believe that banana. Then I make it, and I'm a believer once more. It doesn't matter what sizes of vegetables and fruits you use in the soup; expect the results to be a little different each time. The slower sieve method calls for one more thing: one big commitment to completing the job. When you're finished, if you've been diligent, you should have only one tablespoon of pulp that won't go through the mesh, one powerful forearm, and a singular resolve to invest in a blender. Though yummy served hot, this soup is a cool delight during hot weather.*

1 apple, peeled, cored, and coarsely chopped

1 potato, peeled and coarsely chopped

1 onion, coarsely chopped

1 banana, peeled and cut into 1-inch pieces

1 celery heart with leaves, coarsely chopped

1 teaspoon salt

2 cups homemade chicken stock or canned chicken broth

1 cup light cream or half-and-half

1 tablespoon butter, melted (if serving hot)

1 teaspoon curry powder

Freshly ground white pepper (nice in a white soup)

Snipped fresh chives, for garnish

Put the apple, potato, onion, banana, celery, salt, and stock or broth in a large saucepan and bring to a boil over high heat. Reduce the heat to medium-low and simmer, covered, until the fruits and vegetables are tender, about 20 minutes. Let the soup cool for a few minutes, then force it through a sieve into a large bowl or puree it in batches in a blender or food processor.

Return the soup to the pan and stir in the cream, butter (if the soup will be served hot), curry powder, and pepper to taste. To serve hot, reheat gently over low heat. To serve cold, cool it, then stash it in the fridge. Shower snipped chives over each bowl before serving.

Full-Color Corn Chowder

Serves 2

"How about a 'one-sie two-sie' recipe *once in a while?"* *asked Ellie Hastings, who sets the table for herself most of the time and, now and then, a guest.*

First, make Full-Color Fried Corn (page 209) and eat no more than half of it. Then turn what's left into a folksy chowder with more colors, textures, shapes, bits, and pieces than a patchwork quilt.

LOUDER!
for CORN CHOWDER!

1 sweet potato or yam, baked or boiled and mashed
  At least ½ recipe leftover Full-Color Fried Corn (page 209)
1 cup bouillon, any flavor (1 bouillon cube + 1 cup water)

1 1-pound can cream-style corn
  Handful of grated cheddar cheese or other meltable cheese of your choice
  Salt
  Chili powder

Heat the sweet potato, leftover fried corn, and the bouillon in a large saucepan over medium heat. Don't pick out those cranberries from the fried corn—they're great in there. After a couple of minutes, add the potato, cream-style corn, and cheese. Stir until the cheese melts and the soup is hot. Add salt and chili powder to taste. Thin the soup with water if necessary, and serve hot.

Butternut Squash–Coconut Soup

Serves 6 to 8

Give Sally Bobbitt a pat on the back *for successfully cloning a strange but wonderful squash soup she had tasted at a local restaurant. It looked so odd on paper that it was impossible to resist. Sally likes to drink this soup.* Cook & Tell *loves it thick and spoonable.*

- 1   large butternut squash, peeled, seeded, and coarsely chopped (about 5 cups), or one 20-ounce package frozen butternut squash
- 1   14-ounce can vegetable broth (or 2 vegetarian bouillon cubes + 1³/₄ cups water)
- 1   14-ounce can unsweetened coconut milk (Attention! This is **not** cream of coconut. This is thick, unsweetened coconut milk, found in the Asian food section of the supermarket.)
- 1   teaspoon ground ginger
    Salt

Put the squash and broth in a large saucepan and bring to a boil over high heat. Reduce the heat to medium-low and simmer until the squash is tender, about 10 minutes. Cool to lukewarm. Puree in batches in a blender or food processor. Return the soup to the pan and add the coconut milk, ginger, and salt to taste. Reheat gently over medium-low heat and serve hot, or cool, stash in the refrigerator, and serve cold.

Butternut Squash, Apple, and Stilton Soup

Serves 6

You can combine almost anything *with butternut squash and come up with a hit. A tangy apple and some smooth Stilton, the blue blood of blue cheeses, play a surprising harmony to the satiny melody of butternut squash. Any blue cheese will do, I suppose, but why settle?*

1 medium butternut squash, about 7 inches from stem to stern, peeled, seeded, and coarsely chopped, or one 20-ounce package frozen butternut squash

1 large apple (any kind), peeled, cored, and coarsely chopped

4 cups homemade chicken stock, canned chicken broth, or water

2 tablespoons (¼ stick) butter

2 celery ribs, finely chopped

1 medium onion, chopped

½ cup crumbled Stilton cheese (about 2 ounces)

Freshly ground black pepper

Snipped fresh chives, for garnish (optional)

Put the squash; apple; and stock, broth, or water in a large saucepan and bring to a boil over high heat. Reduce the heat to medium-low and simmer until the squash is tender, about 10 minutes.

Meanwhile, in a medium skillet, melt the butter over medium-high heat. Add the celery and onion and sauté until translucent, about 5 minutes. Add to the squash mixture. When the squash is done, stir in the cheese. Cool until lukewarm. Puree the soup in batches in a blender or food processor. (Hot off the burner, the soup could scald you if the blender surges and overflows.)

Return the soup to the saucepan and gently reheat over medium-low heat. Add pepper to taste; you won't need salt. If the soup is too thick for your taste, thin it with more stock, broth, or water. Serve hot. And if you have nothing else to do, skip out to the herb garden for a bouquet of chives to snip over each serving as a garnish.

Cauliflower and Cheddar Soup

Serves 6

A favorite vegetable dish—*cauliflower crowned with cheese sauce*—*is born again as a soup. Spices lend a hint of the mystical, and the surprise of lemon lifts it above the terrestrial. Bingo! A potful of soulful bowlfuls.*

- ½ medium cauliflower head
- 2 carrots, peeled and cut into chunks
- 6 tablespoons (¾ stick) butter
- 1 medium onion, minced
- 2½ teaspoons curry powder
- ½ teaspoon ground cinnamon
  Pinch of ground allspice
- ½ teaspoon salt
- 3 tablespoons all-purpose flour
- 3½ cups homemade chicken stock or canned chicken broth
- 1 cup grated sharp cheddar cheese (about 4 ounces)
- 1 cup heavy cream, half-and-half, or milk, if you must
  Fresh lemon juice

Separate the cauliflower into two piles: one for the florets and leaves (yes, leaves), and one for the stalk pieces. Cut the florets into chunks and the leaves into pieces and set aside. Cut the stalk pieces into chunks and whir them with the carrot chunks in a food processor until they're in tiny pieces.

In a large, heavy skillet, melt the butter over medium heat. Sauté the stalk-carrot mixture and the onion for about 5 minutes, or until the onion is translucent, 3 to 4 minutes. Process the cut-up florets and leaves into tiny pieces in the food processor and add them to the skillet along with the curry powder, cinnamon, allspice, and salt. Sauté over low heat, stirring often, for 4 to 5 minutes, or until tender but not scorched.

Stir in the flour and cook for about 1 minute, or until the flour is fully incorporated. Transfer the cauliflower mixture to a large saucepan. Raise the heat to high and add the stock or broth gradually, stirring constantly until it comes to a boil. Stir in the cheese until melted, then add the cream, half-and-half, or milk. Reduce the heat to low and cook until slightly thickened, 5 to 7 minutes. Don't let the soup boil, or it will curdle.

Add the lemon juice drop by drop, tasting as you go, until the soup is brightened to your satisfaction. Serve hot.

Prizewinning Yellow Split Pea Soup

Serves 10

Some liked it hot, **some liked it cold.** *Some liked it exotic, some liked it authentically ethnic. But more liked it traditional than any other way. When all was said and sampled, the judges of* Cook & Tell's *first-ever and never-to-be-repeated Pea Soup Olympics awarded the Nobel Peas Prize for Excellence in Soup to* Bob Olsen's *version. Here's everything you always wanted in a split pea soup—a bushel of garden flavors, the mandatory ham bone or hocks, and the fragrance of a country kitchen. It's a revved-up version of a recipe Bob found in the 1976* Grand Rapids Junior League Cookbook.

2   cups dried yellow split peas (1 pound)

2   cups peeled and chopped carrots (about 5 carrots)

2   cups chopped celery with leaves (about 4 celery ribs)

2   cups chopped onions (about 2 large onions)

½   cup chopped fresh parsley or ¼ cup dried

2   teaspoons dried oregano

1   garlic clove, minced

1½   tablespoons salt, plus more if needed

½   teaspoon freshly ground black pepper

1   bay leaf

1   teaspoon sugar

1   meaty ham bone or 2 ham hocks

1   pound kielbasa, cut into bite-size pieces (optional)

Put 8 cups water and all the ingredients except the kielbasa in a Dutch oven or other large, heavy-bottomed pot. Bring to a boil over high heat, stirring frequently. Reduce the heat to low and simmer, covered, for 1½ hours, or until the peas have cooked down into a thick soup. Stir occasionally to prevent sticking. Discard the bay leaf and remove the bone or hocks from the soup. Pick off the meat, chop it coarsely, and add it to the soup. Add the optional kielbasa and heat through. Taste and add more salt if necessary. Serve hot.

NOBEL
PEAS
PRIZE

Wreath of bay laurel leaves and yellow split peas
presented to The Winnah!

Lentil Barley Soup
with Spinach and Prunes

Serves 8

One January I was trying to figure out a theme for the February Cook & Tell, and there were holidays everywhere: presidents' birthdays, Valentine's Day, Groundhog Day, Mardi Gras, and Chinese New Year. Too many possibilities. Finally I just made soup, fiddling my way through a metamorphosis of a lentil soup recipe sent by Ellie Hastings. I changed the quantities, threw out the cheese, threw in spinach. And prunes. I can't blame anyone but myself for the recipe now. It's a good thing it's good.

4 tablespoons (½ stick) butter	1 bay leaf
1 large onion, chopped	Pinch of freshly ground black pepper
2–3 celery ribs, chopped (about 1 cup)	6 cups homemade beef stock or canned beef broth
1 garlic clove, minced	1 10-ounce bag fresh spinach, washed and stemmed
1 28-ounce can chopped tomatoes, with their juice	2–3 carrots, peeled and cut into ¼-inch-thick slices (about 1 cup)
1 cup dried lentils, picked over and rinsed	12 pitted prunes, quartered
1 cup uncooked pearl barley	Olive oil and vinegar (any kind)
1 teaspoon dried rosemary	
1 teaspoon dried oregano	

Melt the butter in a Dutch oven or other large, heavy-bottomed pot over medium heat. Add the onion, celery, and garlic and cook until limp and translucent, about 5 minutes. Add the tomatoes, lentils, barley, rosemary, oregano, bay leaf, pepper, and stock or broth. Bring to a boil over high heat, reduce the heat to medium-low, and simmer, covered, for 45 minutes, stirring occasionally.

Cut the spinach into narrow strips by rolling up several leaves at a time like a cigar and slicing them thinly crosswise. Add the spinach, carrots, and prunes to the soup and simmer until the carrots are tender, 15 to 20 minutes.

Discard the bay leaf and ladle the soup into bowls. Drizzle each bowlful with oil and vinegar and serve.

Sweet-and-Sour Cabbage Soup

Serves 10

Here it is — one terrific cabbage soup. *If you can't bear the thought of bouillon cubes, it could send you searching for a butcher with marrow bones to sell or give away. Made either way, this soup pleases. And it freezes. One thing it hasn't done, through forty years, two husbands, one daughter, and uncounted supper guests, is disappoint.*

1 large cabbage (about 3 pounds; the size of a duck-pin bowling ball), shredded or finely chopped
1 large onion, chopped
1 28-ounce can crushed tomatoes, with their juice
1-1½ pounds meaty, marrowy soup bones or 4–6 beef bouillon cubes

Salt and freshly ground black pepper
2 lemons
About ¾ cup sugar (a mixture of half granulated, half light brown)
Meatballs (optional; see sidebar)

Put the cabbage and onion in a Dutch oven or other large, heavy-bottomed pot and add water to cover. (In my 5½-quart pot, that amounts to 2 quarts water.) Add the tomatoes, bones or, if you're using bouillon cubes, 4 to start, about ½ teaspoon salt, and some pep-

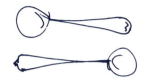

per; you'll be seasoning, adjusting, and tasting over the course of the cooking. Bring to a boil over high heat, squeeze one of the lemons into the soup, and add about half of the sugar mixture. Reduce the heat to low and simmer, covered, for 4 to 5 hours.

Taste the soup from time to time and add more lemon juice and sugar to encourage the winey, sweet-and-sour flavor to develop as the cabbage cooks down. Toss in another bouillon cube, if the spirit moves you (even if you're using soup bones).

Time's up about 5 hours later. The soup will have become a thick slurry of cabbage, in a broth colored russet by the tomatoes, with a perfect balance of flavor, neither lemon nor sugar predominating. Remove the bones. If you want to beef up the soup, raise the heat a bit and drop in a raft of optional meatballs near the end of the cooking, to poach for about 10 minutes (but longer is fine).

Meatballs

I n a large bowl, mix 1 pound ground beef with 1 large egg, about ⅓ cup dry bread crumbs, and salt and freshly ground black pepper to taste. Form the meat mixture into 1-inch balls. Makes about 60 meatballs.

Italian Sausage Stew

Serves 6

In Elfrieda Palmer's potful of pleasures, *the neatly chopped and sliced parts and pieces tiptoe in a puddle of gravy, rather than bathe in a pool. "Is 12 ounces of V8 really going to be enough liquid?" asked Joan Batchelder, calling long-distance. Then, answering her own question as we spoke, she realized that all those veggies, especially the mushrooms, would release lots of juices. But those mushrooms had better be fresh. Jean Ann Biron used the canned kind and had to soup up her stew with chicken broth.*

1 pound sweet Italian sausages (**not** hot)	3 potatoes, peeled and cubed
1 12-ounce can V8 juice	2 cups broccoli florets
3 carrots, peeled and cut into 1-inch pieces	8 ounces white mushrooms, sliced
2 celery ribs, cut into 1-inch pieces	1 tablespoon Worcestershire sauce

Cut the sausages in half, squeeze out the meat, cut it into small pieces, and chuck the casings. Cook the sausage in a medium skillet over medium-high heat until browned, about 5 to 7 minutes; discard the fat, if any. Transfer the sausage to a Dutch oven or other large, heavy-bottomed pot, add the V8, and bring to a boil. Reduce the heat to low and simmer for 5 minutes. Add the carrots and celery and simmer for 10 minutes more.

Add the potatoes, broccoli, mushrooms, and Worcestershire. Simmer until everything is tender, 30 to 45 minutes. Let stand in the fridge overnight before serving (see Note).

🧤 Note 🧤

The stew must rest in the fridge overnight. YOU ARE NOT ALLOWED TO SERVE IT THE DAY YOU MAKE IT, HEAR? I have no idea what will happen if you do, but this is just so darned good, you will not ask questions. A double boiler is a good thing to reheat the stew in, and shallow soup plates are better than deep bowls for serving.

Irish Stew

Serves 6 to 8

Warm and welcoming, *as comforting as they come, this stew's a grand blend of tender lambiness and earthy-sweet vegetables, thickened with barley. The Blue Haven Hotel in Kinsale, Ireland, serves a stew that inspired my version of a country classic that works like insulation against mists and gales.*

"We just had Irish Stew, and it was delicious. Fifteen minutes before it was done, I added parsley and green beans for color. The lamb was so tender (I used a tenderloin), it would melt in your mouth."

— Muriel Jorgenson

2–3 pounds stewing lamb, cut into 1-inch cubes

4 tablespoons (½ stick) butter

4 pounds vegetables, which works out to about:

  2 potatoes, peeled and cut into chunks

  5 carrots, peeled and cut into chunks

  4 celery ribs, cut into chunks

  3 medium onions, cut into chunks

  2 leeks, thoroughly rinsed, trimmed, and cut into 1-inch pieces

  1 purple-topped turnip, peeled and cut into chunks

Handful of uncooked pearl barley

Sprinkle of dried thyme

¾ teaspoon salt

½ teaspoon freshly ground black pepper

1 tablespoon chopped fresh parsley

Blanch the lamb by putting it in a saucepan with cold water to cover and bringing it to a boil over high heat. Immediately remove the lamb with a slotted spoon and set aside in a medium bowl. Skim off foam from the liquid. Reserve 2½ cups of the liquid and freeze the rest for another project.

Melt the butter in a Dutch oven or other large, heavy-bottomed pot over medium-low heat. Add the potatoes, carrots, celery, onions, leeks, and turnip and sauté, stirring frequently, until somewhat limp but not quite tender, about 8 to 10 minutes.

Add the 2½ cups reserved liquid, blanched lamb, barley, thyme, salt, and pepper and bring to a boil over medium-high heat. Skim off the foam. Reduce the heat to low and cook, covered, for about 1½ hours, or until everything is tender. Correct the seasonings, add the chopped parsley, and serve.

## Chapter 2

BEYOND ICEBERG ⨪ arugula · endive · mesclun

Salads of Substance

SALAD DAYS ⨪ Life in the Slaw Lane

TOSSED · JELLED ⨪ OLD, GREEN, LEAFY

arugula · endive · mesclun ⨪ best-dressed list

Caesar Salad

Serves 4

Who remembers the signature *raw egg, now banished from the classic Caesar, that was broken over the salad and then tossed in with such style as to dazzle onlookers? Gone. Anne Andrus's updated Caesar salad is an excellent approximation of the original, and you can make the dressing in advance. Things begin to dazzle when the salad hits your tongue.*

Dressing
- 1 cup olive oil
- 3 tablespoons fresh lemon juice
- 2 tablespoons balsamic vinegar
- 1 tablespoon Dijon mustard
- 1 teaspoon Worcestershire sauce
- 2 large hard-boiled egg yolks
- 1 2-ounce tin flat anchovy fillets, drained
- 1 garlic clove
- 1¼ teaspoons freshly ground black pepper

Salad
- 1 large head romaine lettuce, torn or cut into 1-inch pieces
- ²/₃ cup Easy Homemade Croutons (recipe follows) or store-bought croutons
- Freshly grated Parmesan cheese

To make the dressing: Combine the ingredients in a blender, cover, and whir until thoroughly blended.

To make the salad: Put the lettuce in a large salad bowl. Pour the dressing over the lettuce, sprinkle with the croutons and grated Parmesan, and toss. I have a reputation as a dressing miser, so take my advice or leave it: You may not want to use every bit of this dressing on one bowl of salad.

Easy Homemade Croutons

Makes 2 cups

Don't touch that doorknob! *Get back in here and make your own croutons. You have everything you need, including the time, to produce these lightning-fast toasted cubes for your every salad need. Your humble toaster does most of the work.*

4 slices white or whole-grain bread	½ teaspoon dried thyme
2 tablespoons olive oil	Salt and freshly ground black pepper

Toast the bread in a toaster, cool slightly, then cut into ½-inch cubes. Heat the oil over medium heat in a nonstick skillet large enough to hold the bread cubes in a single layer. Toss in the bread cubes and stir thoroughly to coat with the oil. Sprinkle with the thyme. Cook, stirring and tossing frequently, for 5 to 7 minutes, or until browned on all sides. Sprinkle with salt and pepper to taste. Spread on paper towels to cool.

These croutons get drier and crisper when left on the counter overnight. Stow them in a jar with a tight cover when they can't get any drier.

Fancy, Fancy-Greens Salad
with Raspberry Vinaigrette

Serves 4

Is there anything left to say here? *Camille MacKusick passed along this composition in greens, copied from a swank restaurant's salad offering. It encourages you to pull out all the gourmet stops, starting with a bag of assorted fancy baby lettuces, the only salad-in-a-bag that I'll happily buy. The lacy, miniature leaves raise any salad's chic factor a few notches, and, in this one, dried cranberries provide a chewy, sweet-and-sour contrast. My own rendition of a raspberry vinaigrette is so simple it's embarrassing.*

Raspberry Vinaigrette

- ½ cup raspberry vinegar
- ¼ cup raspberry jam (the kind with seeds is good)
- ¾ cup olive oil
  Salt and freshly ground black pepper

Salad

- ⅓ cup pecan halves
- 1 bag mesclun or assorted baby greens, aka "Spring Mix," washed and spun dry
- ¼ cup crumbled Stilton cheese (about 2 ounces)
- ¼ cup dried cranberries

To make the vinaigrette: Whisk together the vinegar and jam in a medium bowl. Whisk in the oil and salt and pepper to taste. There'll be more than enough dressing for the four salads we're making, which means you'll have some left over. Store in the fridge for up to 2 weeks.

To make the salad: Toast the pecans on a cookie sheet in a pre-heated 300°F oven or toaster oven for 5 minutes, or just until they smell toasty. Keep a hawk's eye on them so they don't burn. Set the pecans aside to cool.

Artfully arrange the greens on four salad plates. Scatter the Stilton cheese evenly over the greens and sprinkle with the cranberries and toasted pecans. Anoint each salad with a judicious amount of dressing. Stand back and sigh before serving.

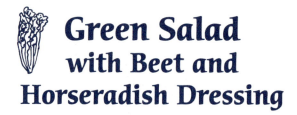

Green Salad with Beet and Horseradish Dressing

Serves 4

For this neat little salad, I thought I had a cucumber on hand, but I was wrong. So I went for the dill pickles to take their place, and they turned out to be sweet bread-and-butter pickles. Either way, or any way, it's a combination that invites fiddling. Don't be surprised if everyone smiles when they see the dollopy dressing. The beets turn it a cheerful, charming pink!

Dressing

- ²/₃ cup sour cream or plain yogurt
- ¹/₂ cup chopped cooked beets (canned are fine)
- ¹/₄ cup finely chopped onion
- 3 tablespoons prepared horse-radish
- 1 tablespoon sugar
- ¹/₂ teaspoon salt

Salad

- About 3 cups torn salad greens of your choice
- 1 medium cucumber, peeled and sliced
- ¹/₄ cup chopped dill or sweet pickles

To make the dressing: Combine all the ingredients in a small bowl and mix well.

To make the salad: Arrange the greens on four plates, divide the cucumber slices and chopped pickles among the plates, and drop thick dollops of the dressing on each salad. Serve immediately.

Eggplant Salad
with Tomato Vinaigrette

Serves 4

The quintessential sopper-upper, *eggplant tastes great baked, then served at room temperature in the company of the piquant, the crunchy, and the juicy, as it is here. The flavorful dressing from Sue Gordon is studded with the kind of tidbits I'd have fought my big brother for when I was a kid.*

1 medium eggplant, trimmed and cut into ³/₈-inch-thick slices
  Olive oil

Tomato Vinaigrette

3 tablespoons olive oil
2 tablespoons balsamic vinegar

2 medium tomatoes, chopped
2 tablespoons chopped Vidalia onion or other sweet onion
4 teaspoons chopped fresh basil or 2 teaspoons dried
1 teaspoon capers, drained
1 garlic clove, minced

Preheat the oven to 425°F.
Brush each eggplant slice with oil on both sides and place on a cookie sheet. Bake for about 20 minutes, or until golden on top. Turn the slices and bake for about 5 minutes more, or until golden. Set aside to cool to room temperature.

To make the vinaigrette: Whisk together the oil and vinegar in a medium bowl. Whisk in the remaining ingredients.

When you're ready to serve the salad, arrange the eggplant slices on a platter (you'll have three or four slices for each serving) and distribute the chunky vinaigrette over them.

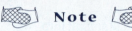 **Note**

Use a bigger eggplant for more salad, and rev up the quantities of vinaigrette ingredients to cover the increase.

Carrot Salad
with Honey Mustard Dressing

Serves 4

It's the dead of winter. *Supermarket tomatoes look—and taste—terrible. The greens are grayish, and the shredded salad fixings in bags are saggy and dreary. What do you do? Try this!*

Dressing

- 1 tablespoon honey
- 1 tablespoon Dijon mustard
- ½–1 teaspoon salt
- 6 tablespoons olive oil
- 2 tablespoons fresh lemon juice

Salad

- 4 carrots, peeled and cut into julienne strips (about 3 cups)
- 2 tablespoons Spanish olives (the kind labeled "salad olives"), chopped
- 2 teaspoons dried currants
- 1 tablespoon snipped fresh chives
- Snipped fresh dill sprigs

"Loved the tangy Carrot Salad. Made it with cashews and regular old raisins. Still great. COOK & TELL recipes invite tinkering."

— Anne Berry

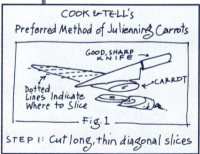

COOK & TELL's Preferred Method of Julienning Carrots

GOOD, SHARP KNIFE

CARROT

Dotted Lines Indicate Where to Slice

Fig. 1

STEP 1: Cut long, thin diagonal slices

Make small piles of slices and cut matchsticks

Voilà!

Fig. 2

STEP 2: Pile 'em up & slice 'em thin

To make the dressing: Whisk together the honey, mustard, and salt in a small bowl. Whisk in the oil, a little at a time, then the lemon juice.

To make the salad: Combine the carrots, olives, currants, chives, and dill in a large bowl and toss with 2 to 3 tablespoons of the dressing. Serve immediately. The leftover dressing will keep for up to 2 weeks in the refrigerator.

Lima Bean Salad

Serves 4

The tidbits in this salad *punctuate pillowy lima beans with a crisp crunchiness and soak up a sparkly citrus dressing improvised by Shirley Gibbs and codified by* Cook & Tell. *No, we didn't forget about oil. There is none.*

Dressing

- 2 tablespoons orange juice
- 2 tablespoons white wine vinegar
- 1 teaspoon honey, or to taste
- ½ teaspoon Dijon mustard
- 1 tablespoon grated fresh orange zest
- 1 tablespoon chopped fresh parsley
- Pinch of dried Italian herb seasoning
- Salt and freshly ground black pepper

Salad

- 1 10-ounce package frozen lima beans (1½ cups), cooked and cooled
- ½ cup finely diced celery
- 2 tablespoons finely diced red onion

Lettuce leaves to line a salad bowl

> ### Note
>
> *If you can't find Italian herb seasoning in jars, use a wee pinch each of thyme, oregano, and sweet basil.*

To make the dressing: Combine the ingredients in a jar, screw on the cover, and shake to blend.

To make the salad: Toss the beans, celery, and onion with the dressing in a large bowl. Transfer to a salad bowl lined with lettuce leaves and serve.

Curried Cole Slaw
with Peanuts and Bacon

Serves 6

"I'm looking for a terrific cole slaw," *wrote Jean Cobb.*
"I'm tired of my usual. I want a showstopper."

OK, Jean, try this. All I can say is, it's spiffy and it's different. Put on a show and see what happens.

½ cup mayonnaise	½ medium cabbage, finely chopped
1 tablespoon sugar	
1 teaspoon curry powder	4 bacon slices, cooked crisp and crumbled
1 teaspoon salt	
2 tablespoons cider vinegar	½ cup chopped salted peanuts

Combine the mayonnaise, sugar, curry powder, and salt in a small bowl. Whisk in the vinegar. Pour the dressing over the cabbage in a large bowl, add the bacon and peanuts, and toss to evenly distribute the goodies. Serve.

"I presented Curried Cole Slaw at a cook-out — not a morsel remained!"

— Lida Iles

Potato and Pea Salad

Serves 6

Memories of a vacation *on Prince Edward Island hover in the kitchen when I make this recipe, inspired by one I clipped from the Boston Globe. I made the salad for the first time shortly before we left on a trip to that tranquil place. So when we discovered acres and acres of rolling farmland all over the island given over to the cultivation of peas and potatoes, it was as if I'd done my homework without realizing it. Back home and back to work on the newsletter, I included the recipe in that month's issue as a companion to Bimby's Best Baked Salmon (page 115).*

4 medium boiling potatoes, cut into matchsticks (or French-fry shapes, which don't take as long to cut)

1 Vidalia onion or other sweet onion, thinly sliced
1 cup cooked peas, at room temperature
¼ cup chopped fresh mint

Dressing
½ cup chopped fresh parsley
½ cup mayonnaise
¼ cup plain yogurt
2 teaspoons cider vinegar
½ teaspoon sugar
   Salt and freshly ground black pepper

team the potatoes in a steamer basket over boiling water in a large saucepan until tender but not falling apart, 5 to 7 minutes, depending on size. Spread them out on a large plate to cool.

To make the dressing: Whisk together the ingredients in a small bowl.

Toss the potatoes, onion, and peas with the dressing in a large bowl. Sprinkle the mint over the salad and serve.

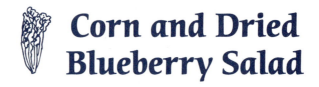

Corn and Dried Blueberry Salad

Serves 6 to 8

This fall salad originated *from a restaurant recipe. Here's where the cheffiness stops. I celebrate the frozen, the dried, and the canned; reverse the restaurant's ratio of orange juice to lime; do away with the vinegar; and switch to southwestern spices.*

Dressing

- ⅓ cup frozen limeade concentrate
- 2 tablespoons orange juice
- 2 teaspoons pure maple syrup
- 1 teaspoon ground cumin
- 1 teaspoon chili powder

Salad

- 2 11-ounce cans white shoepeg corn, drained
- ½ cup dried blueberries
  Lettuce leaves to line a salad bowl

To make the dressing: Combine the ingredients—nope, there's no oil—in a jar. Screw on the cover and shake to blend. Chill for at least 1 hour.

To make the salad: At serving time, shake the dressing again and combine it with the corn and blueberries in a large bowl. Transfer to a salad bowl lined with lettuce leaves and serve.

Perfection Salad

Serves 6

Rise above all those mediocre *molded salads! This one really is perfection, the jewel in the crown of the domestic science movement at the turn of the nineteenth century. It's been showing up in recipe collections for one hundred years.*

1 3-ounce package lemon gelatin	1 piece of pimiento (about 1½
Juice of 1 lemon	by 3 inches), diced
1 teaspoon salt	¼ cup diced green bell pepper
2–3 celery ribs, finely chopped	
(about 1 cup)	Lettuce leaves
3 slices canned pineapple, diced	Creamy salad dressing, such
½ cup shredded cabbage	as Miracle Whip

Dissolve the gelatin in 1¾ cups boiling water in a medium bowl. Add the lemon juice and salt. Chill until the mixture begins to set. Stir in the celery, pineapple, cabbage, pimiento, and bell pepper. Pour into a wet 1-quart ring mold and chill until set. Unmold and serve on lettuce with a creamy dressing. Miracle Whip is perfect!

"Good old Perfection Salad! My mother used to serve it to her card club. She had little molds that said 'Jell-O' on the bottom. She served it on lettuce leaves. I thought that was really thrilling when I was five years old."

—Joanne Jensen

Taco Salad

Serves 6

Remember this one? *You made it years ago, when Fritos were the revolutionary un–potato chip, and a salad starring warm ground beef took some getting used to. Then you forgot all about it and ran off with every pasta salad that came along. But taco salad never went away. It just stayed home, printed in those old community cookbooks and tucked into fat files of clippings, biding its time. So make it now!*

1 pound lean ground beef	½ cup sliced black olives, drained
1 envelope dried onion soup mix	¼ cup chopped green bell pepper
1 medium head iceberg lettuce, shredded (about 4 cups)	1½ cups corn chips, such as Fritos or Doritos
1 cup grated sharp cheddar cheese (about 4 ounces)	Store-bought buttermilk ranch dressing
1 large tomato, cut into wedges	Chili powder
1 small onion, thinly sliced and separated into rings	

Brown the ground beef in a large skillet over medium-high heat. Sprinkle it with the soup mix. Stir in ¾ cup water, reduce the heat to low, and simmer, uncovered, for 10 minutes.

Toss the meat mixture, lettuce, cheese, tomato, onion, olives, and bell pepper in a large salad bowl. Crush the corn chips gently with your hands, add them to the salad, and lightly toss. Drizzle as much dressing as you like over the salad and sprinkle with chili powder to taste. Toss again and serve immediately, while the meat is still warm.

Earthquake Salad

Serves 2

Mary Howard keeps recipes, *including this one from her local paper, in her "earthquake suitcase," along with assorted canned goods and emergency supplies. The folks on Puget Sound in Washington are ever cognizant of the possibility of seismographic friskiness.*

1 1-pound can white beans or chickpeas, drained (cannellini beans are too mushy)

1 6-ounce can solid white tuna, drained

1 2.25-ounce can sliced black olives, drained

¼ cup bottled Italian dressing (or less)

Salt and pepper (the kind in the can — we're talking emergency rations)

Combine all the ingredients, with salt and pepper to taste, in the multipurpose bowl from your earthquake suitcase.

"What a success Earthquake Salad has been! I had to take two dishes to our community pool picnic. I made a double recipe of Earthquake Salad using chickpeas and adding an avocado for glamour. Someone asked for the recipe, and the whole bowl was eaten."

— Christine Crutsinger

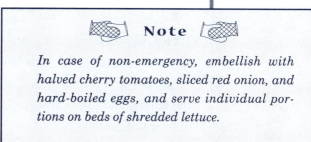

Note

In case of non-emergency, embellish with halved cherry tomatoes, sliced red onion, and hard-boiled eggs, and serve individual portions on beds of shredded lettuce.

Patrice's Fajita Salad

Serves 2; easily doubled

I'm not sure we're talking real fajitas here, *but this salad is "yum-yum-yum," to quote Patrice Robertie. Patrice sampled a dish like this at Pier 66 in Albuquerque, New Mexico, and went home to replicate it. "The sauce starts off medium-hot on your tongue,"* she says, *"but it cools down fast."*

Salad

- 2 boneless, skinless chicken breast halves, cut into pencil-thin strips
- 1/3 cup Basic Vinaigrette (page 56) or store-bought dressing
- 2 tablespoons vegetable oil
- 1 yellow bell pepper, cut into 1/2-inch-wide strips
- 1 red bell pepper, cut into 1/2-inch-wide strips

Dressing

- 1/4 cup mayonnaise (more, if you like)
- 3 teaspoons chipotle chiles in adobo sauce
- 2 teaspoons fresh lime or lemon juice
- 1 garlic clove, minced
  Salt and freshly ground black pepper

To make the salad: Marinate the chicken in the vinaigrette in a medium bowl for several hours or overnight in the refrigerator.

Heat the oil in a large skillet over medium-high heat and sauté the chicken and bell peppers until cooked through, about 5 minutes. Transfer to a serving bowl.

To make the dressing: Combine the mayonnaise, chipotle chiles, lime or lemon juice, garlic, and salt and pepper to taste in a small bowl. Toss with the chicken and peppers. Serve warm.

> ### Note
>
> *Patrice cooks this on her two-piece domed stovetop grill, which sits on a burner. Chipotle chiles in adobo sauce are available in gourmet shops and in the international food aisles of many supermarkets. La Morena is one brand.*

Chicken Couscous Salad

Serves 4

YANKEE magazine once recruited me *to dream up some recipes using the products of one of their advertisers. My assignment was couscous, that teeny-weeny pasta that cooks in no time. Here, the couscous fills in the space between the chicken and vegetables most agreeably and doesn't barge in with a flavor agenda of its own.*

4 boneless, skinless chicken breast halves	¼ cup chopped red onion
2 chicken bouillon cubes	2 tablespoons capers, drained
1 teaspoon butter	¼ cup mayonnaise
½ cup uncooked plain quick-cooking couscous	3 tablespoons orange juice
1 tablespoon sweet rice vinegar	1 orange, peeled, halved, and thinly sliced, or one 11-ounce can mandarin oranges, drained
1 cup frozen baby peas	
¼ cup chopped green bell pepper	Lettuce leaves

Put the chicken, bouillon cubes, and 2 cups water in a medium saucepan and bring to a boil over high heat. Reduce the heat to medium-low and simmer for 15 minutes, or until the chicken is cooked through. Remove the chicken from the stock and let stand until cool enough to handle. Save the stock for another recipe. Shred the chicken into thin strips and set aside.

Combine ¾ cup water and the butter in a medium saucepan and

bring to a boil over high heat. Stir in the couscous and cover. Remove from the heat and let stand for 5 minutes.

Fluff the couscous with a fork and toss with the vinegar. Rinse the frozen peas in a strainer under hot running water until thawed; it will only take a minute or two. Combine the chicken, couscous, peas, bell pepper, onion, and capers in a large bowl. Whisk together the mayonnaise and orange juice in a small bowl and pour the dressing over the salad. Add the orange slices or mandarin oranges and toss gently to blend. Cover with plastic wrap and chill for at least 1 hour. Serve on lettuce leaves.

Couscous and Cashew Salad

Serves 4 to 6

Way back when Cook & Tell *was taking its first timid steps, this salad appeared in the prototype issue I sent to everyone on my Christmas card list and anyone else likely to fall for my subscription pitch. Here we have the updated version, in which I've overthrown the original brown rice and installed fashionable couscous in its place; doubled the orange component; and added cashews and dried cherries.*

Dressing

½ cup vegetable oil

¼ cup orange juice

2 tablespoons fresh lemon juice

1 teaspoon sugar

1 teaspoon salt

¼ teaspoon dry mustard

¼ teaspoon paprika

Salad

1½ cups cooked plain or whole wheat quick-cooking couscous, cooled

2 oranges, peeled, halved, and cut into ¼-inch-thick slices, or one 11-ounce can mandarin oranges, drained

1 cup thinly slivered cabbage

1 celery rib, thinly sliced

⅓ cup dried cherries

4 scallions (white and light green parts), chopped

Celery salt

⅔ cup salted cashews

To make the dressing: Combine the ingredients in a jar, screw on the cover, and shake to blend.

To make the salad: Combine the couscous, orange slices or mandarin oranges, cabbage, celery, cherries, and scallions in a large salad bowl. Sprinkle with celery salt to taste and toss. Pour on as much of the dressing as you like, sprinkle with the cashews, and serve.

Basic Vinaigrette

Makes 1 cup

This is the ultimate *one-size-fits-all salad splash. I found it in an ancient book called* Bettina's Best Salad Dressings, *which was given to me by an antiques dealer who helped in the restoration of our first old house and shared many a meal with us. This is no namby-pamby dressing; it's pungent, assertive. Make it once, then decide whether it might need a garlic clove or a good squirt of ketchup.*

2	teaspoons sugar	$^1/_2$	teaspoon sweet paprika
1	teaspoon dry mustard	$^2/_3$	cup olive oil
1	teaspoon salt, plus more to taste	$^1/_3$	cup cider vinegar

Put the sugar, mustard, 1 teaspoon salt, paprika, oil, and vinegar in a jar, screw on the cover, and shake to blend. Taste and add more salt, if necessary. Use this dressing on your basic tossed greens, in the depression of a half avocado, or drizzled on cold broccoli. It keeps, covered, in the fridge for a week or two.

Blue Cheese Dressing

Makes about 3 cups

Don't buy it, make it! *Using Rita McDonough's formula, you'll have a jarful of true-blue salad dressing in a couple of minutes. But watch out. If your family is anything like Rita's, you'll have them eating it out of the jar. Cover it with a coffee can turned upside down to throw marauders off the scent.*

2 cups mayonnaise	¼ cup cider vinegar
1 cup crumbled blue cheese (about 4 ounces)	2 tablespoons sugar
	1 garlic clove, minced
½ cup sour cream or plain yogurt	

Combine the ingredients in a medium bowl and beat until fluffy. Or, if you like little lumps of cheese in your dressing, mash the cheese with the garlic and about ½ cup of the mayonnaise, then gently stir in the remaining 1½ cups mayonnaise and the remaining ingredients. A wedge of iceberg lettuce is never more elegant than when wearing blue cheese dressing. Store the dressing in the fridge for up to 2 weeks.

Note

For a dandy dip, skip the vinegar.

Mustard Tarragon Dressing

Makes about 1 cup

Pasta salads, **rice and vegetable salads**, *potato salads, and your basic tossed green ones wear this zippy dressing with pride.*

1 tablespoon Dijon mustard	¹/₂ teaspoon freshly ground black pepper
2 teaspoons salt	
2 garlic cloves, halved	³/₄ cup olive oil
1 teaspoon sugar	¹/₄ cup red wine vinegar
¹/₂ teaspoon dried tarragon	

P ut the ingredients in a jar, screw on the cover, and shake to blend. How hard was that? Good for a 2-week sojourn in the fridge.

Thousand Island Dressing

Makes about 1¹/₂ cups

"She was special," *wrote Betty Parker about her mom. "She never ceased to love to read recipes and cook." If you can imagine a ten-cent can of anything, imagine this oldie-but-goodie Thousand Island dressing Betty's mom used to make. The list of ingredients includes some of their quaint prices, circa 1933.*

1 cup mayonnaise	1 10-cent can pimientos,
½ bottle chili sauce (about	drained and chopped
⅓ cup)	(about 2½ tablespoons)
1 15-cent bottle stuffed olives,	1 small onion, chopped
drained and chopped	6 small sweet pickles, chopped
(about ½ cup)	2 large hard-boiled eggs,
	chopped

Combine ingredients. Serve with wedges of iceberg lettuce.

Maple Syrup Dressing

Makes about 1 cup

Here's daughter Amie's favorite dressing. *I don't mean to put words in your mouth, but when you read the recipe, which I found in a folder from some maple syrup outfit, you're going to say, "Why did I ever buy salad dressing? Anybody can make this." Pour the dressing over a red and green cabbage slaw or any leafy salad.*

¾ cup vegetable oil	1 teaspoon salt
¼ cup cider vinegar	½ teaspoon paprika
2 tablespoons pure maple syrup	

Put the ingredients in a jar, screw on the cover, and shake to blend. The fridge keeps it fresh for 2 weeks.

"Maple Syrup Dressing is a champion marinade for salmon."
— Martha Smith

## Chapter 3

Pick it up and pack it up!

Tea under the tree

meals on the move

Good to Go

Take-out munchies

Herb Toasties

Makes 48 toasties

Don't make the mistake *of thinking these toasts from Marion Bates are too dainty for a picnic. They're terrific for every dining event. You make a huge bunch of them, stick them in an airtight tin or jar, and feel rich—until you start actually serving them, and then you weep because they get snapped up so fast. They're the simple sort of thing that makes your reputation.*

8 tablespoons (1 stick) butter, softened
1 tablespoon sesame seeds
1 tablespoon chopped fresh parsley (see Note)
1 tablespoon snipped fresh chives

1 teaspoon chopped fresh tarragon or ½ teaspoon dried
½ teaspoon chopped fresh thyme or ¼ teaspoon dried
12 slices good-quality white or whole wheat bread (I like Pepperidge Farm brand)

Preheat the oven to 325°F.
Combine the butter, sesame seeds, parsley, chives, tarragon, and thyme in a small bowl until smooth. Spread on one side of each of the bread slices. Cut each slice into quarters and put them on an ungreased cookie sheet. Bake on the middle rack for 30 to

Note

If your toasties go wimpy from humidity, a brief respite in a 325°F oven, maybe 5 minutes, will put the starch back into them. You want at least the parsley and chives to be fresh; the other herbs can be dried.

35 minutes, or until the tops begin to color and the bottoms are golden brown. Cool on the cookie sheet; they'll continue to crisp as they cool. Stored in an airtight container at room temperature, the toasties will keep for 5 to 6 days.

Black-Eyed Susan Deviled Eggs

Makes 24 deviled eggs

I don't think I've ever deviled *an egg before the middle of June or after Labor Day, and isn't that stupid? But then, maybe not. Maybe some things just taste better when you're sitting outdoors on a blanket, or indoors when the windows can be wide open. I've hidden an optional secret in each egg and called in Major Grey to flavor the yolks. But he's not the only chutney maker. Use whatever brand, or homemade version, you wish.*

12 large hard-boiled eggs	1 3.75-ounce tin smoked oysters (optional)
1/4 cup mango chutney (cut up any big chunks)	12 pitted black olives, halved crosswise
2 tablespoons mayonnaise	Edible flowers, such as pansies and nasturtiums (optional)
2 teaspoons dry mustard	
1/4–1/2 teaspoon salt	
Chili powder	

Split the eggs lengthwise. Scoop the yolks into a small bowl. Reserve the whites. Add the chutney, mayonnaise, mustard, and salt to the yolks. Mash everything together with a fork until creamy and well blended.

Put a generous pinch of chili powder into each egg white cavity. Drop in an oyster, if using. Pile the yolk mixture evenly into the cavities. Gently poke an olive half into each filled egg. What do they look like? That wild Susan of the black eyes! Or stick a nasturtium or pansy blossom into some of them, for a mildly peppery accent. Serve.

 **Note**

Keep a few of these portable nibblies in your fridge year-round for a quickie off-season picnic or welcome addition to the holiday buffet table.

Rosemary Lemonade

Makes about 5 cups

Tinkerers just can't leave well enough alone *when the subject is lemonade. Their combinations—mint lemonade, watermelon lemonade—are all well and good. But this time we wave the flag for aromatic rosemary, the herb that urges you to remember its piney, Mediterranean disposition when you're squeezing lemons for a tall, cooling drink.*

1 cup sugar

2 teaspoons chopped fresh rosemary or 1 teaspoon dried

Dash of salt

²/₃ cup fresh lemon juice (about 3 lemons)

Combine the sugar, rosemary, dash of salt, and 1 cup water in a small saucepan and bring to a boil over high heat. Reduce the heat to low and simmer for 5 minutes. Remove from the heat.

Combine the lemon juice and 3 cups cold water in a medium pitcher. Strain the sugar mixture into the pitcher; reserve the rosemary. Put the rosemary in a tea infuser to dangle in the pitcher while the lemonade cools in the fridge. Serve cold.

Fancy Iced Tea

Makes about 5½ quarts

This is the perfect brew for weddings *(my mother served it at my own), lawn parties, and assorted special events and warm-weather occasions when a lot of people are going to be thirsty. For just a few, halve the quantities and you're all set to enjoy a picnic and an afternoon tea party on the back porch, with a few glasses left over for cool breaks from gardening chores.*

10	oranges	1	bunch fresh mint
7	lemons	3	cups sugar
1	cup loose orange pekoe tea		

Bring 5 quarts water to a boil in a large pot over high heat. Squeeze the oranges and lemons into a pitcher. Put the orange and lemon rinds, loose tea, and mint in the boiling water. Remove from the heat and let steep for 1 hour. Strain the tea into a large bowl, squeezing the rinds before discarding them. Strain the orange and lemon juice, and add it to the tea with the sugar, stirring to dissolve. Chill and store in pitchers in the refrigerator.

# Consommé
with Crunch for Lunch

Serves 4

If you have room in the back of the fridge *to keep a couple of cans, you'll be ready for a picnic at a moment's notice—or at least you'll be halfway there. Skeptics who turn up their noses at all things jelled and jiggly unless they're sweet, may very well be won over by the delightful crunch factor and the tony topping in this one.*

2 10.75-ounce cans beef consommé with added gelatin, chilled
½ cup finely chopped celery
¼ cup finely chopped scallions (white and light green parts)

2 tablespoons mayonnaise
2 tablespoons sour cream
2 tablespoons crumbled blue cheese

Put the chilled consommé in a medium bowl and fold in the celery and scallions. Stick it back in the fridge until picnic time. Combine the mayonnaise, sour cream, and blue cheese in a small bowl or plastic container and chill. At picnic time, serve the chilled consommé topped with a spoonful of the cheese mixture.

Cold Creamy Borscht

Serves 6

Once we opened the picnic season *with the launch of my husband's canoe on Love's Cove, across the road. I was not allowed to paddle, because I'm supposed to be a lady of leisure (but not until I've made the lunch and cleaned up the kitchen). We pushed off from shore and pulled up at one of the uninhabited islands nearby, sat on a log surrounded by ocean and blue sky, and shared peanut butter sandwiches on whole wheat bread and tin cups of cold borscht. I based my borscht on a recipe from a free Columbo yogurt booklet.*

2 15-ounce cans sliced beets, with their juice

1 small onion, chopped

2 teaspoons sugar

1 teaspoon chopped fresh dill or ½ teaspoon dried

1 teaspoon salt

½ teaspoon freshly ground black pepper

½ cup fresh lemon juice (about 2 lemons)

1½ cups plain yogurt

2 Kirby cucumbers (the bumpy kind for pickling), peeled, seeded, and diced, for garnish

Put the beets, onion, sugar, dill, salt, pepper, and lemon juice in a blender jar and blend until smooth. (You'll probably have to do the blending in two batches.) Pour the puree into a large plastic container with a cover. Stir in the yogurt until well mixed. Chill thoroughly. Pack in your cooler with a separate container of the diced cucumbers to distribute evenly over each cup or bowlful as a garnish. Serve cold.

Our Mothers, Our Mayonnaise

Mayonnaise is a many-splendored thing: a moistener for sandwich fillings, a binder for deviled-egg stuffings, the jump start for a multitude of dips and dressings. Mix it with leftover frozen mixed vegetables for an impromptu salad. Lather a turkey with mayo and roast the bird under a foil tent. Mix it with sour cream, an egg, and some herbs, spread it over fish fillets, and bake. Make a cake with it, for crying out loud!

I was brought up on Hellmann's mayonnaise, the only mayonnaise allowed in the house. As I recall, the word "real" figured prominently in the advertising of this product. My mother bought Hellmann's *Real* Mayonnaise. The implication was clear. Everything else was a fake. Who would have it? So how can I explain how it happened, how years of tradition could be so painlessly expunged from our family history in a moment, without wrenching self-analysis, with no regrets, no looking back?

One day, probably twenty years after I had left the ancestral home to establish a family and home of my own, complete with a pantry stocked with the right, the *real* mayonnaise, I made a startling discovery on a visit to my mother's. There on the door of her fridge was a jar of Cain's mayonnaise, big as life. Hellmann's had been overthrown in a bloodless coup. Incredulous, I asked the matriarch, How come? What the heck, she said, with a shrug of her maternal shoulders. Why not?

Good enough for me. I've bought only Cain's mayonnaise ever since. It was like the end of innocence, only much less frightening. When it's your mother leading you into uncharted territory, you know everything is going to be all right.

 Good to Go

Curry Mayonnaise

Makes about 2 cups

"Do you ever have curry mayonnaise?" asked my role model, nonagenarian Gertrude Burdsall. "Sometimes I make my own mayonnaise with two egg yolks, but often I use Hellmann's Real Mayonnaise to make this always-on-hand sandwich essential." I made it as soon as I put down her letter and have been using it ever since in sandwiches, on hot steamed cauliflower, and as a dip for raw vegetables. It even works with Cain's mayonnaise.

2½ tablespoons fresh lime juice	½ teaspoon ground ginger
1 tablespoon honey	½ teaspoon garlic salt
1 tablespoon curry powder	2 cups mayonnaise

Whisk together the lime juice, honey, curry powder, ginger, and garlic salt in a small bowl. Slowly whisk the lime mixture into the mayonnaise in a medium bowl, using a fork or a flat whisk. Take care not to be too reckless. Beating could break down the mayonnaise and make it thin out. Store, tightly covered, in the fridge for up to 1 month.

make your own

Lime Juice

SPICES

good mayo

honey

curry mayonnaise

Cucumber Sandwiches

Makes 5 whole sandwiches
or 20 triangular quarters

The quintessential teatime sandwich, *the way Miss Betty makes it, may not pass muster with the Brits, who seem to have the patent on cucumber sandwiches. We don't care. We never get hung up on tradition and pedigree; we like all kinds of cucumber sandwiches. This one offers a little more bang per bite than the average cucumber sandwich and goes to picnics as well as tea parties. Make them on the day you plan to eat them, but note the old-fashioned way to keep them fresh in the fridge for a few hours.*

1 medium cucumber, peeled, seeded, and diced (about 1¼ cups)

1 8-ounce package cream cheese, softened

¼ cup finely chopped scallions (white and light green parts) or snipped fresh chives

½ teaspoon garlic salt

½ teaspoon Worcestershire sauce

10 slices good-quality white or whole wheat bread, crusts trimmed (I like Pepperidge Farm brand)

2 tablespoons (¼ stick) butter, softened

Put the diced cucumber in a sieve to drain for about 1 hour. Mix together the cream cheese, scallions, garlic salt, and Worcestershire in a medium bowl until smooth. Fold in the cucumber. Spread 5 of the bread slices on one side with the butter and the remaining 5 bread slices on one side with the cream-cheese mixture. Put together 5 sandwiches with the buttered bread slices on top. Cut sandwiches diagonally into quarters. Pile the quarters onto platters, cover with a slightly damp kitchen towel or paper towels, then with wax paper, and refrigerate until it's time to break them out for afternoon tea or to pack them into a tin for a picnic.

a tisket, a tasket

a picnic in a basket

Clyde's BLT

Serves 1

> **"Dad could never understand** *triangular sandwiches,"* wrote Carolyn Lathrop. *"He didn't like the way things fell out of the corners and the fact that there's nothing to eat when you get to the corners but bread."* Even worse were sandwiches *"piled up in the middle,"* according to Carolyn. *"He hated them. My dad was so wonderful, a great cook, a very funny man."* This is his masterpiece.

- 4 medium-thick bacon slices
- 3 slices good-quality whole wheat bread (not too heavy, with lots of textural interest)
  Mayonnaise, homemade or Hellmann's
- 1 medium tomato, peeled, seeded, and cut into ½-inch dice
- ¼–⅓ cup chopped iceberg lettuce
  Freshly ground black pepper

Cook the bacon in a medium skillet over medium heat until crisp. Drain on paper towels, then crumble.

Sauté 1 bread slice on one side in the hot bacon drippings until golden brown on the bottom, about 2 or 3 minutes. (This middle-layer slice is the big secret of Clyde's BLT). Lightly toast the other 2 slices (the top and bottom of the sandwich) in a toaster.

Now assemble the sandwich, and do it quickly. The sandwich must be hot, the lettuce cold.

Spread one side of each of the 2 toast slices with mayonnaise and sprinkle with pepper to taste.

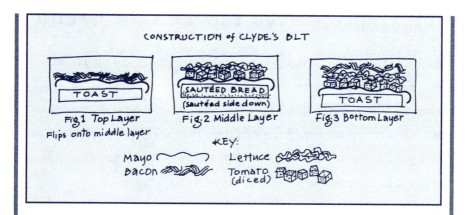

CONSTRUCTION of CLYDE'S BLT

Fig.1 Top Layer
Flips onto middle layer

Fig.2 Middle Layer
SAUTÉED BREAD
(sautéed side down)

Fig.3 Bottom Layer
TOAST

KEY:
Mayo
Bacon
Lettuce
Tomato (diced)

For the middle layer: Spread the *unsautéed* side of the middle-layer toast slice with mayonnaise, sprinkle with pepper to taste, then press half the diced tomato into the mayonnaise. Pile on half of the lettuce.

For the top layer: On the mayonnaise side of one of the toast slices, press half the bacon into the mayonnaise. (The pressing keeps the bits in place.)

For the bottom layer: On the mayonnaise side of the remaining toast slice, press the remaining chopped tomato into the mayonnaise. Cover with the remaining lettuce and bacon.

Put the middle layer, sautéed side down, on top of the bottom layer. Crown the entire construction with the top layer, mayonnaise-and-bacon side down. Nothing will fall off. Cut the sandwich into two rectangles. *Not* triangles. Serve immediately.

Bacon and Egg Salad Sandwiches
on Orange-Rye Coffee Can Bread

Take three dynamic duos — *bacon and egg, carrot and raisin, and celery and onion—unite them all with mayonnaise, spread them on homemade bread, and what have you got? Sandwiches that eat like a real meal, light but satisfying. The quirky, cylindrical loaves will give the yeast-fearing the courage needed to tackle more complicated yeast breads. The no-knead, moist batter bread calls for only one rising.*

Orange-Rye Coffee Can Bread

Makes 2 loaves

1 envelope active dry yeast (**not** quick-rising)	3 cups all-purpose flour
1 tablespoon sugar	1½ cups medium rye flour
⅛ teaspoon ground ginger	1 tablespoon grated fresh orange zest
3 tablespoons molasses	1 teaspoon caraway seeds
2 tablespoons vegetable oil	1 teaspoon salt

Stir the yeast into ½ cup warm water (105° to 115°F) in a large mixing bowl until dissolved. Add the sugar and ginger; let stand for 15 minutes, or until bubbly. Grease well two 1-pound (or 13-to-15-ounce) coffee cans and the undersides of their plastic lids.

Add the remaining ingredients to the yeast mixture. Mix by hand (do not beat) until thoroughly combined. The dough will be moist, like a thick batter. Divide the dough between the coffee cans, cap with the greased lids, and press down to seal. Let rise in a warm place until the lids pop off, about 1 hour. Remove the lids.

Preheat the oven to 350°F.

Bake the loaves for 40 to 45 minutes, or until the tops are golden brown and the loaves begin to pull away from the cans. Let cool in the cans on a rack for 10 minutes. Loosen the crust with a knife if necessary and invert to release the loaves. Cool upright on the rack.

Bacon and Egg Salad Sandwich Filling

Makes enough for 6 sandwiches

5 large hard-boiled eggs, chopped	¼ cup mayonnaise, or to taste
1 carrot, peeled and grated	Salt and freshly ground black pepper
⅓ cup raisins, chopped	
¼ cup chopped onion	12 thin slices Orange-Rye Coffee Can Bread
¼ cup chopped celery	
2 bacon slices, cooked crisp and crumbled	

ombine the eggs, carrot, raisins, onion, celery, bacon, mayonnaise, and salt and pepper to taste in a medium bowl. Cover and chill until it's time to make the sandwiches. Spread the filling thickly on 6 of the bread slices and top with the remaining 6 bread slices. Wrap each sandwich in the original and incomparable picnic wrap, wax paper. Serve cold.

Italian Egg Salad Sandwiches

Serves 6

Andy Blank, Cook & Tell's *man in The Hague, offers this Italian version of egg salad, which he calls "Anchovy Egg Smash." In Italy, it's a popular filler for sandwiches made on soft white bread (with crusts removed) that are sold in bars, gas stations, and airports as tramezzini, or "in-betweeners." Andy uses the mixture as a sauce for leftover cold fish fillets and cold chicken, too.*

3	large hard-boiled eggs	1	tablespoon capers, drained,
3	tablespoons mayonnaise		or chopped fresh parsley
1	2-ounce tin flat anchovy fillets, drained	12	slices soft white bread

Put the eggs, mayonnaise, anchovies, and capers or parsley in a food processor, cover, and whir to a smoothish paste. Spread a spoonful or two—not a lot—between white bread slices. Trim the crusts, cut the sandwiches in half, and serve.

Chicken Tidbits

Serves 4 to 6

Here's a tidy, bite-size finger food *for serving cold, out on the grass in the park, or for serving hot as a supper dish, back home. For picnics, pack the nuggets in a plastic container and pass them around. These tidbits also respond favorably to fork service, which is required for the potato salad (page 82) with which they are quite compatible.*

4 boneless, skinless chicken breast halves, cut into bite-size pieces	¹/₄ cup grated Parmesan cheese
4 tablespoons (¹/₂ stick) butter, melted	1 teaspoon salt
¹/₂ cup fine, dry bread crumbs	1 teaspoon dried basil
	¹/₄ teaspoon dried sage
	¹/₄ teaspoon dried thyme

Preheat the oven to 400°F.

Toss the chicken pieces in the melted butter in a medium bowl to coat. Combine the bread crumbs, cheese, salt, basil, sage, and thyme on a plate and roll the buttered chicken pieces in the bread-crumb mixture until well coated. Put the chicken pieces in a medium baking dish in a single layer (a 10-inch porcelain quiche dish does the trick for me and my 35 morsels). Bake for 20 minutes, or until cooked through. Serve hot or cold.

Melon with Prawns

Serves 4

In a little cookbook *a friend sent me from England, I found a category called "Set Picnics." Here, the author, Prunella Kilbane, presents simple recipes for typically British delicacies, like this one. As in several of her recipes that call for mayonnaise, a certain brand is specified. What a surprise!*

1 medium cantaloupe	Mayonnaise, homemade or
½ pound cooked fresh or frozen prawns (we'll use small shrimp, fresh or canned)	Hellmann's

Slice off and reserve the top from the cantaloupe and cut a piece from the base so it will sit upright on its dish. Discard the seeds and pour off any excess juice. Cut the cantaloupe flesh into small pieces using a knife or melon baller, leaving the rind intact. Combine the cantaloupe with the shrimp in a medium bowl, carefully fold in as much mayonnaise as you like, and spoon the mixture into the empty rind. Replace the top, wrap in plastic wrap so it doesn't flavor other food, and chill until picnic time. Serve cold.

Chef Fritz's German Potato Salad

Serves 4 to 6

Long-time Cook & Tell *subscriber Chef Fritz Blank keeps the fires going at Deux Cheminées, an elegant four-star restaurant in Philadelphia. Every now and then, to lend a little style and a little discipline to the newsletter, he sends me one of his recipes, which are like mini cooking lessons. If I take liberties, I hear about it. Then I confess to the whole readership and promise never to stray again. If you decide to use an oil or vinegar not specified here, I don't want to hear about it.*

1¼ pounds new red or white potatoes (the size of walnuts)

1 tablespoon salt

3 ounces bacon (about 3 slices), cut into ¼-inch pieces

¼ cup thinly sliced scallions (white part only) or ¼ cup chopped onion

3 tablespoons chopped fresh parsley

1 teaspoon coarse salt, plus more if needed

¾ teaspoon freshly cracked black pepper, plus more if needed

½ cup oil mix: the rendered bacon fat plus enough peanut oil to equal ½ cup

¼ cup rice vinegar or mild champagne vinegar, plus more if needed

Put the potatoes and 1 tablespoon salt in a large pot with water to cover by about 4 inches and bring to a boil over high heat. Reduce the heat to medium-low and simmer, uncovered, until the potatoes are tender, about 20 minutes. Be careful not to undercook or overcook. Drain the potatoes and spread them on a tray to cool slightly.

Meanwhile, cook the bacon in a medium skillet over medium heat until crisp but not hard. Drain on paper towels; reserve the drippings. Peel the potatoes while still warm and cut them into $1/4$-inch-thick slices. Put the potatoes in a large bowl and add the bacon, scallions, parsley, coarse salt, pepper, oil mix, and vinegar. Toss gently with your hands, just enough to distribute everything evenly. Do not over-mix.

Let the salad rest for a few hours at room temperature to allow the flavors to blend. Taste and reseason, if necessary, with coarse salt, pepper, and/or vinegar. Serve warm or at room temperature.

Beet and Orange Picnic Salad

Serves 4

"Beet and Orange Picnic Salad is always a hit. I use S&W brand julienne beets, making the prep even easier!"

— Carol Burkholder

Every proper picnic needs *a bit of fancy fork food. We nominate a tasty-tangy beet salad. We love cold beets captured in a jellied ring, tossed with macaroni and mayonnaise, or, as here, spiffed up with unexpected accompaniments. For picnic preparation, pack the dressed beets and onions in a plastic container, the lettuce leaves and walnuts in separate plastic bags, and bring a small can of mandarin oranges and a can opener. You will look so clever when you put it all together.*

1 15-ounce can sliced beets, drained
1 small red onion, thinly sliced
2 tablespoons cider vinegar
1 tablespoon vegetable oil
¼ cup sour cream

Salt and freshly ground black pepper
Tender lettuce leaves (Boston, Bibb, and oak leaf are good)
½ cup canned mandarin oranges, drained
¼ cup chopped walnuts

Slice the beets into julienne strips. Combine them with the onions in a large bowl and toss with the vinegar and oil. Mix in the sour cream and season with salt and pepper to taste. To serve, place the beets on a bed of lettuce in a shallow bowl and arrange the orange sections around the edge. Sprinkle with the walnuts and serve.

Faye's Sour Mustard Pickles

Makes about 1 gallon

Every September, **the gang** *down at the Cozycove Café holds its collective breath in hopes that someone will come through the door with a bushel or a peck of cucumbers, so Chef Gus can make his annual pickles the way Faye Starbird taught him. He won't buy cucumbers, he says, because he gives out these pickles free with every fall sandwich. Well, someone always comes through, and Gus puts up the crisp, vinegary spears that will be ready to eat two weeks later.*

20–22 Kirby cucumbers	6 cups cider or white vinegar
½ cup dry mustard (yes, that's ½ cup)	½ cup sugar
	½ cup pickling or kosher salt

Wash the cucumbers and quarter them lengthwise. Stuff them into a gallon-size glass or plastic jar. Dissolve the dry mustard in about 2 cups of the vinegar in a large, nonreactive bowl, then add the sugar, salt, remaining 4 cups vinegar, and 2 cups water. Whisk until the sugar and salt are dissolved, but don't heat the mixture. Pour the brine over the cucumbers in the jar, right up to the top. If there's any brine left over, pour it into a smaller jar over any quartered cucumbers that wouldn't fit into the big jar. No processing! The pickles are ready in about 2 weeks, but they're great right away, too. They keep in the fridge for about 10 weeks.

> **Note**
>
> *Your local deli or restaurant should be able to supply you with an empty gallon-size glass or plastic mayonnaise jar.*

Lime-Honey-Marinated Fruit
in a Jar

Serves 4

Raid the fruit bowl, *add some specimens bought especially for the occasion, and bathe everything in a sweet-and-sour dressing for a snazzy little extra to dress up a plate of cold chicken. Packed in a jar with a good screw-on lid, it will look as pretty as jewels.*

Dressing

- 2 limes
- 1 cup vegetable oil
- ⅓ cup honey
- 1 tablespoon poppy seeds
- ½ teaspoon paprika
- ½ teaspoon dry mustard
- Dash of salt

Salad

- ½ pineapple, trimmed and cut into bite-size pieces
- 1 apple, cored and cut into bite-size pieces
- 1 cup seedless grapes
- 1 cup strawberries, halved or quartered if large

To make the dressing: Grate the zest of 1 lime and combine it with the juice of the 2 limes, the oil, honey, poppy seeds, paprika, dry mustard, and salt in a jar. Screw on the cover and shake to blend. You'll have enough dressing for this salad as well as a few more.

To make the salad: Shortly before embarking on your excursion to picnic paradise, put the pineapple, apple, strawberries, and grapes in a large bowl and toss to mix. Fill a 1-quart jar with the fruit to within an inch or so of the top and pour in dressing to fill. Cover and gently tilt the jar back and forth to distribute the dressing. Do it again before serving. Consider any fruit that didn't fit in the jar fair game for a sneak attack on the fridge later. Store the leftover dressing in the refrigerator for up to 2 weeks.

 **Note**

Don't rule out melon cubes, peach slices, and grapefruit sections. You can also take a banana along to the picnic site to peel, cut up, and add to the salad when you get there.

Raspberry Bars

Makes 20 bars

For picnics, **we leave raspberry tarts** *to the fancy folks,
and roll up our sleeves and roll out bars instead. These sweetly simple
bars showed up in a travel article about Prince Edward Island in the
Christian Science Monitor years and years ago. They make me think
of lupines growing along roadsides for as far as you can see.*

1¼ cups all-purpose flour
 1 teaspoon baking powder
¼ teaspoon salt
½ cup vegetable shortening
 1 large egg
 1 teaspoon milk (a teeny amount
   that matters!)
¾ cup raspberry jam

Topping
½ cup granulated sugar
½ cup packed light brown sugar
 2 tablespoons (¼ stick) butter,
   softened
 1 large egg
 1 teaspoon vanilla extract
1¼ cups shredded coconut
 1 tablespoon all-purpose flour

Preheat the oven to 350°F. Grease a 9-inch square or a 7-by-11-inch baking pan (sometimes called a brownie pan).

Sift together the flour, baking powder, and salt in a large bowl. Cut in the shortening with a pastry blender or 2 knives. Add the egg and milk, blending well with a spoon until you can gather the dough in a mass. Pat the dough evenly into the pan. Bake for 10 minutes. Spread the jam over the hot pastry.

To make the topping: Combine the granulated sugar, brown sugar, and butter in a medium bowl. Add the egg, vanilla, coconut, and flour and blend well. Drop the coconut mixture by spoonfuls over the jam and spread to cover. Bake for 20 to 25 minutes more, or until the top is golden. Cool before cutting into 20 bars, carefully running a sharp knife around the edges, where the jam may have leaked out. Store in a covered tin for up to a week or in the freezer for up to 2 months.

Mock Moravian Sugar Cakes

Makes 24 "cakes"

Here comes Marion B. again, *with a plate of sweets for a tea party. It's folksy cinnamon toast that grew up and got sophisticated! With this recipe and a loaf of bread, teatime is never more than a half-hour away.*

1 cup sugar
1 tablespoon ground cinnamon
8 tablespoons (1 stick) butter, melted

8 thin slices good-quality, day-old white bread, crusts trimmed (I like Pepperidge Farm brand)

Preheat the oven to 300°F.
Combine the sugar and cinnamon in a pie plate or shallow bowl. Put the melted butter in a separate pie plate or shallow bowl. Cut the bread slices into thirds. Dip both sides of the bread pieces in the butter, then press both sides into the cinnamon-sugar, coating as thickly as possible. Put the bread pieces on an ungreased cookie sheet and bake for 20 to 25 minutes, or until golden brown. Serve warm. They're still swell when thoroughly cool, when they're a little bit chewy, like cookies.

have yourself a yummy little supper

The Real Meal

No-Fault, No-Meat Menus

Top o' the meal to you!

REAL MEAL

Have some more

FINISH YOUR DINNER or THERE'S NO DESSERT

Poultry & Meat

Fish

Meatless

Bacon-Wrapped Stuffed Chicken Breasts with Simplest Chicken Gravy

Serves 6

Chicken tastes just like chicken, *no matter what you do to it. But if you want to make it mysterious, charge its straightforward flavor statement with hidden meaning, like a stuffing of whole prunes. Serve these roll-ups hot, in a pool of gravy, or serve them cold, sliced to reveal their secrets. The thinnish gravy makes a good puddle to park the chicken on.*

6 boneless, skinless chicken breast halves
   Salt and freshly ground black pepper
2 tablespoons Dijon mustard

12 pitted prunes
9 bacon slices, halved lengthwise
   Simplest Chicken Gravy (recipe follows)

Preheat the oven to 350°F.
   Put the chicken breasts on a cutting board and lay a piece of wax paper over each one. Pound each chicken breast gently with a wooden mallet or the bottom of a heavy pan to flatten slightly. (This will make the stuffing and rolling easier.)

Sprinkle the chicken all over with salt and pepper to taste, then spread one side of each piece with mustard. Place two prunes in the center of the mustard-coated side of each piece. Roll it into a tidy mound, covering one prune first, then rolling some more until the second prune is tucked in. Lay 3 half-slices of bacon on the cutting board

chicken breast wrapped in bacon
chicken→
bacon→
PLAN VIEW Fig 1.
(Note braided effect)

and place a chicken bundle on top, seam side down. Pull the bacon strips a bit to stretch them out. Crisscross them over the top of the chicken bundle and secure the whole works with a toothpick. Repeat the steps for the remaining chicken breasts. Place the stuffed chicken breasts in a shallow baking pan. Bake for about 35 minutes (longer for more well-done bacon), or until the chicken is cooked through. Remove the toothpicks and serve with Simplest Chicken Gravy.

Simplest Chicken Gravy

Makes 1 cup

1 tablespoon butter
1 tablespoon olive oil
1 tablespoon all-purpose flour

1 cup homemade chicken stock
  or canned chicken broth
  (a bouillon cube and a cup
  of water will do)
½ lemon
  Salt (optional)

Melt the butter with the oil in a small saucepan over medium heat. Add the flour and stir for 1 minute. Add the stock or broth and stir until the gravy boils and thickens. Give it a brief squeeze of lemon. Season to taste with salt, if necessary.

◁Ψ◎⋈ Quaker Chicken

Serves 6

What fun, to get all the credit *for a gorgeous, golden brown chicken like this, all glistening and aromatic, when so little effort is required to prepare it. Chris Conant thinks she heard somewhere that this is a method the Quakers use. While the chicken's in the oven, there's plenty of time to fix a vegetable, make mashed potatoes, and put a salad together.*

1	4-pound chicken	5	sprigs fresh rosemary or
2	teaspoons olive oil		1 tablespoon dried, or
			5 sprigs fresh tarragon or
			1 tablespoon dried

Preheat the oven to 375°F.

Rinse the chicken inside and out and pat dry with paper towels. Poke the chicken all over with a sharp fork and brush it with the oil. If using a fresh herb, finely chop 3 of the herb sprigs and pat all over the chicken. Tuck each of the remaining 2 sprigs between a drumstick and the body. If using a dried herb, pat it all over the chicken.

Roast the chicken in a small roasting pan—you don't need a rack—for about 1¼ hours, or until a drumstick wiggles easily and the juices run clear. Don't bother to baste it. You'll have some lovely juice to start a soup or gravy. Serve hot.

Auntie's Tender Pork Chops

Serves 4

I never heard Auntie say *"Maybe" or "This way might work."*
She firmly proclaimed, "This is how you do it." So, when a Cook &
Tell *reader begged to be told how to cook pork chops "tender and juicy,*
not hard and dry," Auntie sure enough told her. If you don't like
breaded chops, Auntie says to skip the milk and bread crumbs and
follow the same method. Although I have never done that, I do not
doubt her.

  This is what you serve with Auntie's Tender Pork Chops: Fried
Sweet Potatoes (page 150) and Broccoli-Cheese Pseudo Soufflé
(page 147).

Salt	½ cup evaporated milk
4 pork chops, any cut, boneless or bone-in	¾ cup fine, dry bread crumbs
	2–3 tablespoons vegetable oil

Lightly salt the pork chops on one side only and let stand, lightly
covered, for 1 hour. Put the evaporated milk in a shallow bowl
and put the bread crumbs in another. Dip the chops first into the milk
and then into the crumbs, coating thoroughly. Heat the oil in a large
skillet over medium-high heat and brown the chops on both sides,
about 5 minutes. Reduce the heat to low, cover, and cook until tender,
25 to 35 minutes, depending on the thickness of the chops. Serve
immediately.

"Thanks to Auntie for her pork chop advice. For the first time ever, Allan likes pork chops."

—Laura White

Amie's Good Meat Loaf

Serves 6 to 8

"Amie's Good Meat Loaf is like my mother's. She would center a hard-boiled egg in it. This always confused our children, who were told by their father that the egg boiled in the meat loaf. They could never figure out what happened to the shell."

—Alice Peters

COOK & TELL gets a kick out of *being some distance from the cutting edge. But we must admit to a certain smugness when we find ourselves in front of, instead of behind, the* New York Times. *The issue of* Cook & Tell *touting this recipe had been in circulation for two weeks when the Sunday food pages of the* Times *turned up with four meat loaf recipes featured. Even the* Times's *title, "Not Your Mother's Meat Loaf," could have described Amie's recipe—Amie is my daughter. Her recipe source was her stepbrother, who got it from a swank eatery where he worked. Daughter, then mother, made adjustments to this great meat loaf, with its presautéed onion and built-in ketchup.*

1 tablespoon olive oil	1 teaspoon Worcestershire sauce
1 small onion, chopped (about ½ cup)	1 teaspoon soy sauce
2 garlic cloves, minced	½–1 teaspoon Tabasco sauce
1 teaspoon dried thyme	¾–1 teaspoon salt
1½ pounds ground beef	½ teaspoon freshly ground black pepper
¼ cup fine, dry bread crumbs	
1 large egg	
¼ cup ketchup	

P reheat the oven to 400°F.

Heat the oil in a large skillet over medium heat and sauté the onion and garlic until limp and translucent, about 5 minutes. Add the thyme and sauté for 1 minute more. Set aside to cool.

Combine the ground beef, bread crumbs, egg, ketchup, Worcestershire, soy sauce, Tabasco, salt, and pepper in a large bowl. Add the onion mixture and combine. Pack the beef mixture into a 1½-quart glass loaf pan. Bake for 45 minutes, or until the juices from a dainty slit made by a sharp knife are no longer pink. Let stand for 5 minutes, slice into slabs, and serve.

Family Favorites

Amie's Good Meat Loaf
Hokey's Roast Potatoes
Full-Color Fried Corn
Grandma Schmidt's
Apple Pie

My Own Gourmet-Style Meat Loaf

Serves 12

"My Own Gourmet-Style Meat Loaf has been voted our most favorite meat loaf of all time."

—Judith Woodbury

Once there was a little *hole-in-the-wall café where the meat loaf was so good that the owner and chef refused to give out the recipe. When cold, it held together nicely for clean slicing. Smeared with ketchup and surrounded by bread, it changed the meaning of "meat-loaf sandwich" for me. I tried my darnedest to copy the chef's meat loaf, veering off from a recipe in* Gourmet, *until my version was so good I couldn't remember what hers tasted like anymore.*

2 tablespoons (¼ stick) butter

1 bunch scallions (white and light green parts), chopped

1 small onion, finely chopped

2 celery ribs, finely chopped

2 garlic cloves, minced

1½ teaspoons dried thyme

2 cups finely chopped white mushrooms (a processor does a fine job on these)

2 teaspoons salt

1 teaspoon freshly ground black pepper

1 10-ounce package frozen chopped spinach, thawed and squeezed out by handfuls until practically bone-dry

1½ pounds ground beef

¾ pound ground pork

1 cup fresh whole wheat or white bread crumbs

2 large eggs, lightly beaten

½ cup chopped fresh parsley

4 bacon slices, halved lengthwise

P reheat the oven to 350°F.
Melt the butter in a large skillet over medium heat. Sauté the scallions, onion, celery, garlic, and thyme until limp and translucent, about 5 minutes. Add the mushrooms, salt, and pepper and sauté for 5 to 10 minutes more, until the mushroom juices evaporate. Stir in the spinach.

Transfer the mushroom mixture to a large bowl and let cool slightly. Add the beef, pork, bread crumbs, eggs, and parsley. Dive in with your hands and mix until well combined. Pack as much of the meat mixture as will fit into a 1-quart glass loaf pan. Form the remaining meat mixture into a tidy oval and plunk it into a pie plate. Drape the bacon strips over both loaves. Bake the larger loaf for about 70 minutes, the smaller for about 60 minutes, or until cooked through. This way, you'll have one loaf to eat hot and the other one to slice, cold, for sandwiches.

Meatball Stroganoff

Serves 4 to 6

Written on a three-by-five file card *in the distinctive up-and-down script of my mother, this recipe dates back to the time when store-bought sour cream was big news and chafing-dish cookery was turning housewives into hostesses. It's a period piece that makes the transition to your double boiler with ease and is as yummy as ever.*

Meatballs

1½   pounds ground beef
1   medium onion, finely chopped
¼   cup fine, dry bread crumbs
1   garlic clove, minced
1   teaspoon salt
    Pinch of freshly ground black pepper
½   cup milk
3   tablespoons vegetable oil

Sauce

1   cup sour cream
¼   cup all-purpose flour
1   10.5-ounce can beef consommé
3   tablespoons Worcestershire sauce
1   6-ounce can sliced mushrooms, drained

Hot cooked noodles

To make the meatballs: Combine the ground beef, onion, bread crumbs, garlic, salt, pepper, and milk in a large bowl. Gently shape the beef mixture into 1-inch balls.

Heat the oil in a large skillet over medium-high heat and brown the meatballs well, about 6 minutes. Reduce the heat to low and cook until the meatballs are no longer pink in the middle, about 8 minutes, turning frequently. Drain off the fat and set aside the meatballs in a bowl.

To make the sauce: Whisk together the sour cream and flour in the top of a double boiler. Whisk in the consommé and Worcestershire. Set the top of the double boiler over the bottom, full of boiling water. Add the meatballs and mushrooms and cook, covered, until heated through. Serve over hot noodles.

⊲Ψ◻ℵ Empanada

Serves 6

Line up, **companeros**, *for a toothsome hunk of meat pie. A peek at the ingredients might make you think "chili," and if the thought just won't go away, go with it. Empty a can of beans and a can of tomatoes into the mixture and to heck with the pastry. The rest of us gauchos, however, will have ours as written, between two crusts. Some of us may even stuff the filling into little circles of pastry, fold and crimp them, and then call them empanaditas, a friendly, diminutive version.*

1–2	tablespoons vegetable oil (optional; use if the beef is lean)	¹/₄ cup chopped black olives
1	pound ground beef	¹/₄ cup chopped pimiento-stuffed green olives
1	medium onion, chopped	About ¹/₄ cup ketchup
2	tablespoons chili powder	Pastry for a double-crust 10-inch pie (see Fail-Safe Piecrust, page 311)
2	teaspoons ground cumin	
	Dash of salt	¹/₄–¹/₂ cup raisins

Preheat the oven to 450°F.
Heat the oil, if using, in a large skillet over medium-high heat. Add the ground beef, onion, chili powder, cumin, and salt and sauté until the beef is browned and the onion is limp and translucent, about

5 minutes. Add the olives and enough ketchup to make the mixture glisten wetly, but not enough to make it runny.

Roll out half of the pastry and use it to line a 7-by-11-inch baking pan, pressing the pastry up the sides of the pan about 1 inch. Spread the beef mixture over the pastry and sprinkle with the raisins. Roll out the remaining pastry for a top crust, lay it over the filling, seal, and crimp the edges with a fork.

Bake for 15 to 20 minutes, or until the crust is golden. Cool for 15 minutes for best cutting—6 squares for main-course servings, 12 for snacks or if you're putting on a big spread with lots of other selections. You can serve the empanada warm or at room temperature. It responds well to reheating, too.

Meat 'n' Potatoes Moussaka

Serves 9

It's snowing. *The kids will return from sledding soon, and their tummies are rumbling. If it's after 4:30 and you're anything like my mother, they won't get anything to eat except a raw carrot, or it'll spoil their supper. When this cheesy, custard-topped casserole comes out of the oven, they'll be glad they waited.*

Allison Corbett added a layer of potatoes to Cook & Tell's *version to pacify a skeptical relative who considered himself a meat-and-potatoes man.*

¼ cup olive oil
5 medium potatoes, peeled and cut into ¼-inch-thick slices
½ teaspoon salt
3 medium eggplants, peeled and cut into ¼-inch-thick slices

Meat Sauce
2 tablespoons (¼ stick) butter
2 large onions, chopped
2 pounds ground lamb
1 garlic clove, minced
3 medium tomatoes, diced
1 8-ounce can tomato sauce

½ cup chopped fresh parsley
1 teaspoon ground cinnamon
1 bay leaf
   Salt and freshly ground black pepper

Cheese Sauce
2 tablespoons (¼ stick) butter
¼ cup all-purpose flour
2 cups milk
1 cup cottage cheese
1 cup freshly grated Parmesan cheese
3 large eggs, lightly beaten

Preheat the oven to 400°F. Brush a 9-by-13-inch baking pan with 1 teaspoon of the oil.

Cook the sliced potatoes in a large saucepan of boiling salted water until barely tender, about 8 to 10 minutes. (They'll be baking in the casserole.) Brush 2 cookie sheets with the remaining oil (you may need 3 sheets). Put the eggplant slices on the cookie sheets and bake for about 8 minutes, or until lightly browned. Flip the eggplant slices and bake for 6 to 8 minutes more, or until lightly browned on the other sides. Set the eggplant slices aside on the cookie sheets and reduce the oven temperature to 375°F.

To make the meat sauce: Melt the butter in a large skillet over medium heat and sauté the onions until limp and translucent, about 5 minutes. Add the lamb and garlic, stirring to break up the meat. Add the tomatoes, tomato sauce, parsley, cinnamon, bay leaf, and salt and pepper to taste. Cook, stirring occasionally, until the sauce is very thick, about 30 minutes. Set aside.

To make the cheese sauce: Melt the butter in a medium saucepan over low heat. Whisk in the flour and cook, whisking constantly, for 1 minute. Gradually whisk in the milk. Raise the heat to medium and, whisking constantly, bring to a boil and boil for 1 minute. Cool slightly, then whisk in the cottage cheese, Parmesan, and eggs.

To assemble: Lay half of the baked eggplant slices in the baking pan. Cover with half of the parboiled potato slices. Sprinkle lightly with salt and pepper to taste. Spoon on half of the meat sauce. Repeat the layers, using the remaining eggplant, potatoes, and meat sauce. Pour the cheese sauce over the top. Bake for about 45 minutes, or until golden brown.

 Note

This gets better and better every day, but don't think of freezing it. The potatoes go all funny if frozen.

Cider Pot Roast ◁𝄞▣⦚

Serves 6 to 8

THE recipe to take with you *if you knew you'd be stuck on a desert island for the rest of your life. Oh, and take a head of red cabbage with you, and a can of corn and some frozen lima beans, too, so you can make Red Cabbage with White Grape Juice (page 218) and Plainest and Best Succotash (page 145).*

1½	cups apple cider	1	3-to-4-pound beef chuck roast
1	tablespoon light brown sugar		All-purpose flour
2	teaspoons salt	2	tablespoons vegetable oil
¼	teaspoon ground cinnamon		
¼	teaspoon ground ginger		Hot mashed potatoes
2	whole cloves		

"My husband is not a fan of standard pot roast, but this one is the exception. The gravy is amazing."

— Ann Bambrick

Combine the cider, brown sugar, salt, cinnamon, ginger, and cloves in a medium bowl. Put the beef in a 1-gallon zipper-lock bag and pour in the marinade. Let marinate in the fridge for 24 hours, jiggling the bag whenever you think of it.

> ▩ **Note** ▩
>
> *Thicken the gravy, if you'd like, with 2 tablespoons all-purpose flour and ½ cup tepid water shaken together in a covered jar and whisked into the simmering juices.*

Remove the beef from the marinade; reserve the marinade. Dredge the beef in the flour on a large plate. Heat the oil in a Dutch oven or flameproof roasting pan over high heat and brown the beef on all sides, about 15 minutes. Reduce the heat to low, add the reserved marinade, cover, and simmer for 3 hours, or until very tender. Let the roast rest for 10 minutes, then slice and serve with hot mashed potatoes.

Veal Goulash
Austrian

Serves 6

Years ago, when I first *made this dish, you couldn't find the kind of exquisite Hungarian paprika you can now, and capers were borderline weird. Introduced to me by my mother-in-law, who was half countrywoman and half sophisticate, veal goulash became the featured attraction at many a supper party. Thin buttered noodles are the traditional accompaniment. Add Fancy, Fancy-Greens Salad with Raspberry Vinaigrette (page 36) and finish off the meal with Turkish Apricot Dessert with Pistachios and Whipped Cream (page 276). Your guests had better be worth it.*

3	tablespoons butter		Salt
3	medium onions, chopped	2	large tomatoes, chopped
2	pounds stewing veal, cut into small cubes	1	3-ounce jar capers, with their juice
3	tablespoons good-quality sweet paprika	1	cup sour cream (more, if you like)

Melt the butter in a large skillet over medium heat and sauté the onions until limp and translucent, about 5 minutes. Add the veal, paprika, and salt to taste, and brown over medium-high heat until no more pink shows, about 10 minutes. (The meat won't really brown; it will "gray.") Add the tomatoes, reduce the heat to low, and simmer, covered, until the veal is tender, 1½ to 2 hours. Add the capers, adjust the seasoning if necessary, and cook, partially covered, until the sauce has thickened, about 1 hour. At the last minute, gradually stir in the sour cream. Serve immediately.

Note

Stewing veal is not always easy to find. Check it out with your local supermarket meat manager first, keep your eyes peeled when you're shopping out of town, or, when all else fails, consult a specialty butcher shop.

◁ᵞ☐ᵺ Smoked Cod Pie

Serves 6

In the course of conducting research *for an issue on Irish food, I found the recipe for this tasty pie. A good fish market is the place to find smoked cod, and it's also available from many specialty food mail-order catalogs. For an all-Irish menu, serve with County Clare Vegetable Soup (page 12), Braised Celery and Carrot (page 210), and Irish Oat Scones (page 308).*

2 tablespoons (¼ stick) butter, plus more for the pie plate
1 pound smoked cod, haddock, or pollack
1½ cups milk
1 medium onion, chopped
2 heaping tablespoons all-purpose flour
1 teaspoon dry mustard
1½ cups frozen baby peas
3 cups hot mashed potatoes (4 potatoes mashed with milk and butter)
Paprika
Chopped fresh parsley, for garnish

Preheat the oven to 400°F. Butter a 9- or 10-inch pie plate. Put the fish and milk in a medium saucepan over medium heat. Bring to a boil. Reduce the heat to low and simmer for 10 minutes. Remove the fish from the milk; reserve the milk. Flake the fish, discarding the tough edges. Set aside.

Melt the 2 tablespoons butter in a medium skillet over medium heat and sauté the onion until limp and translucent, about 5 minutes. Stir in the flour and mustard. Add 1 cup of the reserved milk (the cat will love the rest) and cook, stirring, until thickened. Add the fish and frozen peas (the sauce will seize up when those cold peas are introduced, but it will get back on track in a jiffy as the peas cook) and cook, stirring, for 2 minutes, or until the peas are heated through. Transfer the fish mixture to the pie plate, cover with the mashed potatoes (you may not want to use all 3 cups), and lavish paprika over the top. Bake for about 30 minutes, or until the potatoes are lightly browned. Sprinkle with a ton of good green parsley and serve.

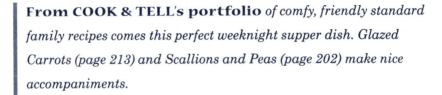 # Scalloped Salmon

Serves 6

From COOK & TELL's portfolio *of comfy, friendly standard family recipes comes this perfect weeknight supper dish. Glazed Carrots (page 213) and Scallions and Peas (page 202) make nice accompaniments.*

Butter
½ cup milk
½ cup homemade chicken stock
    or canned chicken broth
2 large eggs, lightly beaten
½ cup finely chopped celery
¼ cup chopped fresh parsley or
    2 tablespoons dried
2 tablespoons chopped onion
1 teaspoon Dijon mustard

1 15-ounce can red salmon,
    drained
2 cups grated cheddar cheese
    (about 8 ounces)
2 cups herb-seasoned croutons
    or stuffing mix
1 tomato, thinly sliced
1 teaspoon snipped fresh chives
1 teaspoon chopped fresh
    parsley

Preheat the oven to 350°F. Butter a 9-inch pie plate.
Combine the milk, stock or broth, eggs, celery, parsley, onion, and mustard in a large bowl. Add the salmon, cheese, and croutons or stuffing and stir to blend. Transfer to the pie plate and bake for 35 to 40 minutes, or until golden brown For the last 5 minutes of baking, arrange the tomato slices in a ring on top of the scalloped salmon. Sprinkle with the chives and parsley and serve hot in wedges.

Bimby's Best Baked Salmon

Serves 4

Bimby Conant and her husband *come to Southport Island from Atlanta every summer. The Maine accent and the southern drawl mix congenially in Bimby's cooking; there'll be lobster boats on the cove, and grits and salmon on the menu. For a cool accompaniment on a warm summer evening, trot out Potato and Pea Salad (page 44) and, for dessert, Eleanor's 1921 Lemon Sherbet with Hot Blueberry Sauce (page 198).*

4 1-inch-thick salmon steaks	Salt and freshly ground
3 tablespoons chopped fresh	black pepper
dill weed or 2 teaspoons	1 lemon, plus 4 thin lemon
dried	slices, for garnish

Preheat the oven to 350°F.
Wipe the salmon steaks with a wet paper towel and pat them dry with paper towels. Sprinkle on one side only with the dill and salt and pepper to taste. Squeeze the lemon over the steaks. Place on a rack in a baking pan, then place the pan on the lower rack of the oven and bake for 20 to 25 minutes, depending on thickness, or until pale pink and dry inside when tested with a knife. Do not turn them at all. Not even once, hear? Serve immediately with a lemon slice on each steak.

Barbecued Salmon

Serves 4

"Simple and simply wonderful."

—Pam Pingree

Gather around, boys and grills! *Light 'em up and let's get cookin'! Pam Pingree from Alaska sent in this winner.* Cook & Tell *spent a lot of time trying to figure out what made her barbecue sauce special. Hint: nutmeg.*

- 1½ 1-pound salmon fillets, skin on
- ½ teaspoon salt
- ¼ teaspoon freshly ground black pepper
- ⅛ teaspoon garlic powder
- ½ cup mayonnaise
- 2 teaspoons prepared mustard (any kind)
- 1 small onion, thinly sliced and separated into rings
- Barbecue Sauce (recipe follows)

Preheat the grill.

Sprinkle the fleshy side of the fillet with the salt, pepper, and garlic powder. Mix the mayonnaise and mustard in a small bowl and spread on the same side of the fillet.

Cook the fillet, flesh side down, on a covered grill for 7 minutes. Keep a squirt bottle of water at the ready for flame dousing, in case of drippy mayonnaise. Turn the fillet flesh side up. Scatter the onion rings over the fish and cover it lightly with foil. Grill, covered, for 15 minutes more, or until the flesh flakes with a fork. Serve with warm Barbecue Sauce.

Barbecue Sauce

Makes a little over 2 cups

2 cups ketchup
1 tablespoon Dijon mustard
3 tablespoons light brown sugar
1 teaspoon Worcestershire sauce

¼ teaspoon ground nutmeg, or more to taste
½ teaspoon seasoned salt (Lawry's, lemon-dill, or your favorite)

Combine the ingredients in a medium bowl, cover, and heat in the microwave until warm. Stir and serve on the side.

"No, no, no! It's never too cold to grill!"

— Mary Hartnett

BACKYARD BARBECUE

Barbecued Salmon
Summer Corn Casserole

Chef Fritz's German Potato Salad

Fresh Strawberry Pie

Curried Cauliflower Jacket Potatoes

Serves 4

In London we ran into *"jacket potatoes" in all the little sidewalk restaurants and sandwich shops. The British fluff up a whole baked potato and pour over it things like chicken and cheddar cheese or baked beans and sausages, resulting in a tasty square meal similar to our own stuffed baked potatoes. I devised this version in remembrance of the great Indian cuisine we enjoyed at the Regent Tandoori, near Piccadilly Circus.*

Concoct the curried cauliflower while the potatoes are baking.

4   cups cauliflower florets, cut into bite-size pieces
3   tablespoons vegetable oil
1   green bell pepper, cut into narrow strips
1   small onion, halved from stem end to root end, then thinly sliced in the same direction

4   teaspoons curry powder
2   medium tomatoes, coarsely chopped
2   tablespoons ketchup
2   tablespoons plain yogurt
4   hot, freshly baked potatoes
    Salt

Steam the cauliflower in a steamer basket in a large saucepan of boiling water until barely done, about 5 minutes. Set aside.

Heat the oil in a large skillet over medium heat and sauté the bell pepper and onion until the onion is limp and translucent, about 5 minutes. Reduce the heat to low, stir in the curry powder, and sauté for 1 minute more. Add the tomatoes and sauté until the tomatoes fall apart, about 5 minutes. Add the steamed cauliflower and sauté for 2 minutes more, then stir in the ketchup and yogurt.

With a fork, pierce the top of each baked potato in a crisscross pattern and break it open by pushing the ends toward the middle. Fluff the potato flesh with the fork, sprinkle with salt to taste, and top each with an overflowing portion of the curried cauliflower. Serve immediately.

SANDWICH MAN AT GIOVANNI'S, LONDON

ENGLISH EATEN HERE

GRANARY BAPS

SWEET TROLLEY
Apple Flan ·2.
Carrot Cake ·

Three-Grain Casserole

Serves 6 to 8

Becoming familiar with a universe *of grains, spices, and lesser-used vegetables can tap a hitherto unknown vein of creativity. In this recipe, grains and beans combine in an efficient way, familiar to vegetarians, to produce what's called a "complete protein." It tastes good, too.*

2 tablespoons vegetable oil

8 ounces white mushrooms, coarsely chopped

2 carrots, peeled and thinly sliced on the diagonal

1/4 cup chopped onion

1 garlic clove, minced

1/2 cup uncooked pearl barley

1/4 cup uncooked brown rice

1/4 cup uncooked coarse-grind bulgur

1 1-pound can black beans, drained

1 11-ounce can whole-kernel corn, drained (see Note)

1 1/4 cups homemade vegetable stock or canned vegetable broth (or 2 vegetarian bouillon cubes + 1 1/4 cups water)

1 teaspoon soy sauce

1/2 cup grated Monterey Jack or cheddar cheese (about 2 ounces)

Preheat the oven to 350°F.

Heat the oil in a large skillet over medium heat and sauté the mushrooms, carrots, onion, and garlic until the onion is limp and translucent and the mushrooms are juicy, about 5 minutes. Stir in the barley, rice, and bulgur and cook for 1 minute more. Add the beans

and corn and transfer the mixture to a 1¹/₂-quart casserole dish. Stir in the stock or broth and soy sauce and cover tightly. If you use foil, be sure to crimp it smartly. Bake for 60 to 70 minutes, or until the grains are tender, stirring once halfway through the baking.

Remove from the oven, uncover, and sprinkle with the cheese. Cover again and let stand outside the oven for about 5 minutes, or until the cheese is melted. Serve hot.

Note

I always prefer white shoepeg corn to yellow corn. If you can only find the shoepeg variety frozen, it will be just dandy in this long-cooking casserole. Put it right in, frozen.

 # Jim's Pizza

Serves 1 or 2

Jim Hansen's pizza takes *the big deal out of the pizza proce-dure. There's virtually no kneading or rising. You end up with a Frisbee-size pizza with just the right thinness and chewiness. Kids can make these. Singles will love them. So what are we waiting for?*

½ teaspoon vegetable oil	4–5 white mushrooms, sliced
⅔ cup all-purpose flour	¼ cup chopped onion
⅓ cup wheat germ	¼ cup chopped green bell
1 envelope active dry yeast	pepper
1 teaspoon sugar	⅓–½ cup grated mozzarella,
¼ teaspoon salt	fontina, or Monterey Jack
¼ cup C&T's Official Pizza Sauce	cheese, or a combination
(recipe follows)	of any or all

Preheat the oven to 475°F. Oil a 9-inch pie plate.

Put the flour, wheat germ, yeast, sugar, salt, and 6 tablespoons water in a medium bowl and stir until a ball forms. Knead ever so briefly, just until all the flour is assimilated. On a floured board, roll or pat out the dough into a circle to fit the prepared pie plate, with a little going up the sides to form an embankment. Spread with the pizza sauce and arrange the mushrooms, onion, and bell pepper over the sauce. Sprinkle the cheese over the top. Bake for 10 to 15 minutes, or until the cheese is gooey and the crust is as brown as you like it.

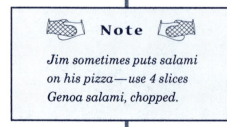 **Note**

Jim sometimes puts salami on his pizza—use 4 slices Genoa salami, chopped.

C&T's Official Pizza Sauce

Makes about 3 cups; enough for 12 pizzas

This recipe makes a lot of sauce, *so refrigerate or freeze what you don't use right away.*

2	tablespoons olive oil	3	8-ounce cans tomato sauce
1	small onion, chopped	1	tablespoon sugar
2	garlic cloves, minced	1/2	teaspoon dried oregano
1/4	cup tomato paste		Salt and cayenne pepper

Heat the oil in a medium saucepan over medium heat and sauté the onion and garlic until limp and translucent, about 5 minutes. Stir in the tomato paste and cook for 3 minutes more. Add the tomato sauce, sugar, oregano, and salt and cayenne to taste. Bring to a boil and simmer, uncovered, for 20 minutes. The sauce will keep, tightly covered, in the refrigerator for up to 2 weeks or in the freezer for up to 6 months.

◁Ψ◎▯⋈ Mushroom Burgers

Serves 5

Here, **the mammoth fungus** *of the hour and a host of culinarily correct ingredients politely conspire to bring you a super alternative to ordinary burgers. Cashews take a bow, but use whatever nuts are at hand, if you like.*

Judith Woodbury raved about the recipe, even though, she said, "It didn't 'burger.'" She had been shy with the yogurt and mayonnaise binder, so she happily served the mixture as hash.

¹/₃ cup uncooked fine- or medium-grind bulgur

1 tablespoon vegetable oil

8 ounces portobello mushrooms or white mushrooms, finely chopped

1 bunch scallions (white and light green parts), chopped

1 carrot, peeled and minced

3 garlic cloves, minced

1 cup fine dry bread crumbs (see Note)

¹/₂ cup ground cashews or other nuts

1 tablespoon soy sauce

1 teaspoon prepared mustard (any kind)

Plain yogurt

Mayonnaise

Ketchup or tartar sauce (optional)

C ombine the bulgur and ²/₃ cup water and let stand for 35 minutes, or until the bulgur absorbs the water.

Heat the oil in a large skillet over medium heat and sauté the mushrooms, scallions, carrot, and garlic until the carrot is soft and the mushrooms are juicy, 6 to 8 minutes. Remove from the heat and stir in the bulgur, bread crumbs, cashews, soy sauce, and mustard. Add 2 to 3 tablespoons yogurt and about the same amount of mayonnaise — whatever it takes to achieve a manageable patty texture. If the mixture gets too soft and floppy, you'll need more bread crumbs;

better to err on the side of crumbly and then add yogurt and mayonnaise cautiously. Form the mixture into 3-inch-wide patties about ½ inch thick. Broil on a greased cookie sheet in the oven or toaster oven,

 **Note**

If a search of the pantry and fridge fails to turn up bread crumbs, cut 8 slices of bread into cubes; bake on an ungreased cookie sheet at 350°F until totally dry, about 15 minutes; and whir them in the blender.

turning once, for 5 to 6 minutes, or until browned on both sides. Serve hot, with ketchup or tartar sauce, if desired.

Cheese 'n' Chutney Portobello Pitas

Serves 4

Ever notice how those great big *portobello mushroom caps almost exactly match the mini pita breads in size? When my neighbor wondered what to do with portobellos, I adapted a recipe from a women's magazine, sending in a whole portobello cap to replace the suggested chopped white mushrooms. Think lunch! Think hors d'oeuvres! Think how tasty!*

> *"Put the sautéed portobello cap gill-side up on the pita pocket, to collect all the cheese and chutney."*
>
> — Sherrie Groman

¼ cup olive oil

4 tablespoons (½ stick) butter

4 portobello mushroom caps

½ cup grated Swiss cheese (about 2 ounces)

½ cup crumbled Stilton cheese (about 2 ounces)

4 small pita breads

¼ cup mango chutney (cut up any big chunks)

Preheat the oven to 400°F.

Heat the oil and butter in a large skillet over medium-high heat and sauté the mushrooms, turning frequently and pressing down with a spatula, for 7 minutes, or until tender and juicy. If you want to be absolutely sure, sneak a teeny-weeny wedge of a mushroom and taste it for doneness. Combine the cheeses in a small bowl. Sprinkle 1 tablespoon of the cheese mixture on each pita bread; this will anchor the mushrooms to the pitas. Set a mushroom cap on top of each pita, gill side down. Sprinkle each pita with 3 tablespoons of the remaining cheese. Bake for 5 minutes, or until the cheese is bubbling and browning at the edges. Drizzle each pita with 1 tablespoon chutney. Cut the pitas into halves or quarters and eat them with your fingers.

## Chapter 5

◇·Speedy·Eats·◇·Expeditious·and·Delicious·◇

Cook It Easy

◇·A·Meal·a·Minute·◇·Go-Go·Galley·Goodies·◇

Hasty·Tasties·◇·Chef·Presto's·Best

Good·Chow·Fast·◇·Fast-Track·Snacks

◆COOK IT *Easy*◆

Listen up!

CHARM SCHOOL

~ where the crockpot gets a hearing
and cans & mixes gain respectability

Fanny's Corn Chowder

Makes 6 to 8 servings

Joanne Jensen's favorite chowder *comes from a now-defunct combination café and shop where lunch was served in antique bowls on antique tables. If you could pay the price, you could walk off with the furniture. This recipe makes immense demands on your can opener, but remember: Sometimes that's a good thing!*

2 bacon slices, cooked crisp and crumbled	1 10.75-ounce can condensed cream of celery soup
1½ cups diced cooked chicken or ham	1 14.5-ounce can chicken broth
½ cup minced onion	1 1-pound can cream-style corn
⅛ teaspoon dried thyme	½ cup sliced canned tomatoes
	1 6-ounce can sliced mushrooms

Put every single thing in a medium saucepan. And don't ask whether to drain the tomatoes and mushrooms. I don't. What does it matter? Heat and serve.

Tip

Paul Dupuis likes to thicken "white" chowders with instant potato flakes.

Tomato Fish Chowder

Serves 4

You should keep all these *ingredients on your pantry shelf at all times—even the clam juice, which comes in handy in fishy things and transforms tomato juice into a gourmet elixir—so that all you have to do is run out to the fish market for a pound of haddock and, presto: a fine kettle of fish!*

1 10.75-ounce can condensed cream of tomato soup	½ teaspoon dried basil
1 14.5-ounce can stewed tomatoes, with their juice	1 pound haddock or cod fillets, cut into bite-size pieces
1 8-ounce bottle clam juice	A few shakes of Worcestershire sauce

Combine the tomato soup, stewed tomatoes, clam juice, and basil in a large saucepan over medium-high heat. Bring almost to a boil, reduce the heat to low, add the fish, and simmer, stirring occasionally, until the fish is cooked through, about 7 minutes. Season to taste with the Worcestershire and serve.

 # Pantry Pasta

Serves 2

Between the pantry, *the vegetable bin, and the fridge, you're going to find everything you need to make Judi Wagner's pasta supper for two. We like to use orzo, a rice-shaped pasta. If you want to break out of the grated-cheese rut, use a vegetable peeler to produce interesting cheese shavings for the topping.*

1 carrot, peeled and thinly sliced or finely chopped

½ cup chopped broccoli

½ cup chopped cauliflower

1 cup uncooked orzo or your favorite pasta

Salt

2 tablespoons olive oil

1 medium onion, chopped

1 garlic clove, minced

A few white mushrooms, sliced

1 14.5-ounce can stewed tomatoes, drained (reserve 2 tablespoons of their juice)

1 14-ounce can artichoke hearts, drained

¼ cup grated or shaved Parmesan or Romano cheese (about 1 ounce)

⅓ cup pitted black olives

Cook the carrot, broccoli, cauliflower, and pasta in a large pot of boiling salted water for 8 minutes, or until everything is tender. Drain.

Meanwhile, heat the oil in a large skillet over medium heat and sauté the onion and garlic until limp and translucent, about 5 minutes. Add the mushrooms and sauté until they soften and give up their juices, about 5 minutes. Add the tomatoes and artichokes and sauté for 1 to 2 minutes more, or until heated through. Add the 2 tablespoons reserved tomato juice and the pasta mixture and toss to distribute everything evenly. Dole it out into bowls and top each serving with 2 tablespoons cheese and a few olives.

 **Note**

You may use any combination of carrots, broccoli, and/or cauliflower or skip them altogether. For the sautéed portion, you may add sliced red or green bell pepper and skip the mushrooms.

# Roman Pie

Serves 6

No kid on earth *is going to turn down a plate of Marge Eaton's friendly, yummy casserole. Topped with highly American potato chips, it also features melty Velveeta! When Marge was well into her eighties, she was still serving this to her bridge club and miscellaneous luncheon guests.*

1 tablespoon butter, plus more for the baking dish	8 ounces processed American cheese, such as Velveeta, cubed
1 cup broken-up uncooked spaghetti	2 large hard-boiled eggs, coarsely chopped
Salt	1 3-ounce can button mushrooms, drained
1 onion, chopped	1 1.75-ounce bag potato chips, for the topping
½ green bell pepper, chopped	
1 14.5-ounce can tomatoes (plain, stewed, whole, sliced, whatever)	

Preheat the oven to 350°F. Butter a 1½-quart baking dish or a 9-inch pie plate.

Cook the spaghetti in a large pot of boiling, salted water until al dente, about 6 minutes. Drain and return to the pot.

Meanwhile, melt the 1 tablespoon butter in a large skillet over medium heat and sauté the onion and bell pepper until the onion is limp and translucent, about 5 minutes. Add to the cooked spaghetti.

Stir in the tomatoes, cheese, eggs, and mushrooms. Transfer the mixture to the prepared dish. Lightly crush the potato chips in the bag and sprinkle on top of the pie. Bake until bubbling and beginning to brown around the edges, about 1 hour in a baking dish or 45 minutes in a pie plate. Serve hot.

Nesbitt
(Macaroni Casserole)

Serves 4

OK, so nobody likes fish, *and chicken has gotten boring. Then make Nesbitt. Totally untrendy, it's the consummate gang's-all-here or summer-cottage supper (it doubles easily). Priscilla Talley's family named it for the Misses Nesbitt, who brought the dish to them every year upon the Talleys' arrival at their summer place.*

	Butter	1	14.5-ounce can diced tomatoes,
1	cup uncooked elbow macaroni		with their juice
2	tablespoons vegetable oil	1½	cups grated cheddar cheese
1	medium onion, coarsely		(about 6 ounces)
	chopped		Pinch of sugar
			No salt!

Preheat the oven to 350°F. Butter a 1- or 1½-quart baking dish. Partially cook the macaroni in a large saucepan of boiling water, about 7 minutes. Drain and return to the pot.

Meanwhile, heat the oil in a medium skillet over medium heat and sauté the onion until limp and translucent, about 5 minutes. Add the sautéed onion, tomatoes, cheese, and sugar to the drained macaroni and stir gently but thoroughly. Transfer the mixture to the prepared baking dish (it will be loose and wet). Bake for 45 minutes, or until bubbling and nicely tightened up. Serve hot.

Fast and Fabulous Dump Casserole

Serves 4

From Susan Delaney-Mech, *a chemist with a knack for combining elements, comes a perfectly simple casserole with a simply perfect blend of flavors. When the dinner bell rings on the night this dish is scheduled, be there.*

"It's the simplest recipes that are the best."

—Andy Blank

4 boneless, skinless chicken breast halves
³/₄ teaspoon dried basil
Salt and freshly ground black pepper
1 6-ounce can pitted black olives, drained

1 15-ounce can tomato sauce (preferably Hunt's tomato sauce with tomato bits, onions, celery, and green bell peppers, or a reasonable facsimile; plain tomato sauce will do)
2 tablespoons olive oil

Preheat the oven to 350°F.
Put the chicken in a casserole dish with a cover. Sprinkle with the basil and salt and pepper to taste. Dump in the olives. Dump the tomato sauce on top. Drizzle with the oil. Cover and bake for 1¹/₄ hours, or until fork tender. Serve hot.

The 20-Minute Supper

A working mother with a family *of mostly males to feed, Phyllis Gim-bel developed the 20-minute supper for the times when the gang is panting for food and you've just raced in the door from work.*

Shape 1½ pounds of ground chuck into a loaf and slice it into thick slabs. Brown some sliced onions, add a can of drained mushrooms, push them to the side, and brown the beef slices on both sides. Smother it all with a jar or two of Heinz brown gravy and simmer until the patties are cooked through. Serve with instant mashed potatoes and a veggie. "Corn and beets are surprisingly good and ready in no time. People think buttered beets are wonderful," says Phyllis.

Ann's FAST Turkey (or Chicken) Bake

"A no-brainer for a busy day" *is how subscriber Ann Fawcett describes a dish that deserves far more than that. I suggest a string of glowing adjectives like "delicious" and "delightful." Post this recipe on the fridge door for regular reference.*

Preheat the oven to 350°F. Mix together a 1-pound can of whole-berry cran-berry sauce and 1 packet onion soup mix. Pour the mixture over 3 pounds turkey or chicken parts (like thighs and drumsticks) in a roasting pan or Dutch oven. Cover and bake for 2 hours. The meat will obligingly fall off the bones.

Swedish Meatballs
with Corn Chips

Serves 4

We'd been having a continuing *flap over what, exactly,*
makes a meatball Swedish. Some said allspice; others nutmeg. Then
Christine Crutsinger remembered her mother-in-law's meatballs,
which purport to be Swedish, but which give off not even a whiff of
either spice. But that's OK. We're all just glad that the Vikings discov-
ered Fritos in their journeys.

A little less than 1 pound
    ground beef

1 cup corn chips, such as Fritos,
    crushed

1 5-ounce can evaporated milk

1 large egg

Salt and freshly ground
    black pepper

2 tablespoons vegetable oil

1 10.75-ounce can condensed
    cream of mushroom soup

Hot egg noodles

Combine the ground beef, corn chips, evaporated milk, egg, and a pinch of salt and pepper in a large bowl. Form into rounded patties (they cook faster than balls). Heat the oil in a large skillet over medium-high heat and brown the patties on both sides, about 5 minutes. Pour the soup and 1 can hot water over the patties. Reduce the heat to low and simmer, covered, for 20 minutes. Uncover and simmer for 5 to 10 minutes more, or until the sauce is thickened. Serve hot over egg noodles.

Spareribs
and Sauerkraut

Serves 4

You just cannot do this one wrong. *You don't have to drain the sauerkraut. You don't even brown the ribs; they brown without your help. The recipe was handed down to Camille MacKusick by her father-in-law, from the family archives. All sorts of magical juices ooze out of everything. When the last finger is licked and the last lip smacked, everyone will weep.*

8 country-style spareribs	About one-half 18-ounce
1 1-pound can sauerkraut,	bottle barbecue sauce
drained	No salt, no freshly ground
	black pepper!

Preheat the oven to 300°F. Choose a baking pan that will accommodate the ribs in pieces or all hitched together, with the kraut in the space left over. Eight country-style ribs cut into a 6-rib and a 2-rib hunk, plus the can of kraut, fit perfectly in a 9-by-13-inch pan. For more ribs, get a bigger pan and more kraut.

Place the ribs in the pan and the sauerkraut in a mound beside them. Cover the ribs—not the kraut—with the barbecue sauce. Use as much as you like, maybe more than half the bottle, maybe less. Cover the pan tightly with aluminum foil and bake for 3 hours. Lift a corner of the foil near the end of the time to sneak a look. The ribs should be nicely browned and glazed and your mouth should water. Serve hot.

RIBS & KRAUT
Fig. 1

Showing placement of
8 country-style ribs and
sauerkraut in baking pan
before applying BBQ sauce.
(Plan view)
A. Ribs
B. Kraut

Fig. 2
Pan of ribs covered
with foil, ready to bake.
(Elevation)

 # Pork Stir-Fry

Serves 6

No need to call for Chinese take-out. *We've got the classic dish right here. It could be your fall-back answer to the question, "What am I going to make for dinner tonight?" as well as your automatic response to invitations to potlucks and other adventures in group eating. Like all good Chinese take-out, it's great left over, so double the recipe and store the remains in the freezer, to, well, take out later. A thin pork steak works well, and so does leftover roast pork. The quantity you use depends on whether you're big on meat or bigger on vegetables.*

¼–½ pound lean boneless pork, cut into small cubes
3 tablespoons vegetable oil
4 cups finely slivered cabbage
2 medium green bell peppers, thinly sliced
2 large onions, chopped
4 medium carrots, peeled and cut into 1½-inch-long matchsticks
Salt and freshly ground black pepper
Hot cooked rice
Soy sauce

Heat a large, heavy skillet over medium-high heat and cook the pork cubes without oil, tossing frequently, until cooked through, about 5 minutes. If using leftover roast pork, skip this step and wait until you've drained the water from the mixture and are finishing off the dish before adding the pork. Transfer the cooked pork to a bowl and set aside.

Heat the oil in the skillet over medium-high heat and stir-fry the cabbage, bell peppers, onions, and carrots for 2 to 3 minutes, or until barely tender and still crunchy. Add water to cover, mix well, and drain quickly. Return the skillet to medium-high heat and add salt and pepper to taste. Stir-fry until the vegetables are crisp-tender, 3 to 5 minutes more. Add the reserved pork (now's the time to toss in the leftover roast pork, if using) and stir-fry until heated through. Serve hot with the rice, splashed with the soy sauce.

Tomato Aspic

Serves 4

What kind of a world was it *before Jell-O and canned tomatoes, especially the tomatoes with celery, green bell peppers, and onions added? And lemon Jell-O.*

1   14.5-ounce can stewed tomatoes, including the juice
1   3-ounce package lemon gelatin
1   tablespoon Worcestershire sauce

Lettuce leaves or shredded iceberg lettuce
Mayonnaise or creamy salad dressing, such as Miracle Whip

Break up the tomatoes coarsely with two knives, right in the can, and empty them into a small saucepan. Add the gelatin and stir to soften it. Heat gradually over medium-high heat, stirring constantly to be sure the gelatin is thoroughly dissolved. Stir in the Worcestershire. Pour into a wet mold or bowl and chill until set. Serve in wedges, squares, or slices on lettuce leaves or shredded iceberg lettuce, with mayonnaise or salad dressing. Small cubes of the aspic are a nifty topping for a tossed green salad.

Plainest and Best Succotash

Serves 4

Pay attention, *or this one will get past you. It's just so darned good and shamelessly simple, I can't stand it. Ann McFarlin passed along the recipe from Nancy Wood, who styled her succotash from her aunt's. Both Ann and Nancy are very definite about these complex directions. Do not mess with them.*

- 1 10-ounce package frozen Fordhook lima beans (not, repeat **not**, baby limas)
- 1 11-ounce can white shoepeg corn, drained

Hunk of butter
Salt and freshly ground black pepper

Cook the limas in a medium saucepan as the package directs, then drain. Add the corn to the limas and throw in a generous hunk of butter. Add salt and pepper to taste. Working quickly, give it a stir, cover, and let the heat from the limas warm the corn, but do not let the succotash actually *cook*. Set aside on a warm burner until you're ready to serve.

Chinese Asparagus

Serves 4

Bias-cut and sautéed *in oil is how Pat Parker cooks the slender stalks. But don't overcook. You want them to be crisp-tender.*

1 pound asparagus
1 tablespoon vegetable oil
Pinch of salt

Pinch of freshly ground
black pepper

Snap off and discard the woody ends of the asparagus stalks. Cut the asparagus on an acute diagonal into ¼-inch-thick slices.

Heat the oil in a large skillet over high heat. Add the asparagus, salt, and pepper. Cover and shake the skillet as if you were shaking a wire popcorn popper, cooking until the asparagus is barely tender, 3 to 4 minutes. Serve hot.

Broccoli-Cheese Pseudo Soufflé

Serves 6

For ages, my husband, Bob, *has campaigned vigorously on behalf of Cheez Whiz as a broccoli enhancer, and I have resisted. I never liked the stuff. So wasn't he thrilled when I finally caved in and bought a jar to make Pauline Burrill's "soufflé," a recipe that somehow grabbed me. I enjoyed it as much as he did. But that's all we're ever going to do with Cheez Whiz (unless some other intriguing conglomeration comes to my fickle attention).*

6   tablespoons (¾ stick) butter or margarine, plus more for the casserole dish

¼   cup finely chopped onion or 1 tablespoon dehydrated minced onion

6   tablespoons all-purpose flour

1   6-ounce jar processed American cheese sauce, such as Cheez Whiz

2   10-ounce packages frozen chopped broccoli, thawed and well drained

2   large eggs, well beaten

½   cup crushed saltines or buttery crackers, such as Ritz

Preheat the oven to 325°F. Butter a 1½-quart casserole dish. Melt 4 tablespoons of the butter in a medium saucepan over medium heat and sauté the chopped onion, if using, until limp and translucent, about 5 minutes, or stir the dehydrated onion into the melted butter. Stir in the flour and $1/2$ cup water and cook until thickened, about 30 seconds. Stir in the cheese sauce. Stir the broccoli into the sauce and remove from the heat. Cool briefly, then add the eggs and mix gently. Pour the mixture into the prepared dish and cover with the cracker crumbs. Dot with the remaining 2 tablespoons butter. Bake for about 45 minutes, or until bubbling. Serve hot.

Rice Pilaf Supremo

Serves 4

I can't believe how good this is, *notwithstanding the Minute Rice, which I snatch off the supermarket shelf only when nobody's looking. Double the quantities for extravaganzas, where this dish will shine. With "supremo" in its name, you just know it's going to be good.*

1⅓ cups uncooked quick-cooking rice, such as Minute Rice

1 10.75-ounce can condensed French onion soup

1 3-ounce can button mushrooms, drained

3 tablespoons butter, cut into chunks

½ teaspoon freshly ground black pepper

⅓ cup dried cranberries

Combine the rice, soup, mushrooms, butter, and pepper in a 1-quart microwavable baking dish. Cover and microwave on high for 5 minutes. Stir in the cranberries, cover, and microwave on medium for 5 minutes more. Let the casserole stand, covered, for several minutes before serving.

> ### Note
>
> *To make this on top of the stove, combine the soup, mushrooms, butter, pepper, and cranberries in a medium saucepan over medium-high heat and bring to a boil. Add the rice, cover, remove from the heat, and let stand for 5 minutes, or until all the liquid has been absorbed. Fluff up with a fork and serve immediately.*

Fried Sweet Potatoes

Serves 3 or 4

"Fried Sweet Potatoes are a favorite at Thanksgiving and Christmas in my husband's family in the north Idaho panhandle."

— Joanna Allen

A relentless search for food thrills *is my excuse for applying peanuts and scallions to a no-nonsense dish from my mother that is perfectly, pristinely good in its unglamorized state. She, however, would never have authorized the inclusion of such foreign matter.*

3 tablespoons vegetable oil, plus more if needed

1 29-ounce can whole sweet potatoes or yams, drained and cut into ½-inch-thick slices

2–3 scallions (white and light green parts), chopped

Handful of salted peanuts, chopped

Heat the oil in a large skillet over medium-high heat and fry the sweet potatoes or yams, turning them carefully as they brown. A little burned is good, but please, not enough to set off the smoke alarm. Add more oil if they start to stick. When the sweet potatoes or yams are heated through and artfully browned, about 6 to 8 minutes, serve with a flurry of scallions and peanuts.

Note

If it's October and you're into theme cooking, make and serve this in a black cast-iron skillet for a certain orange-and-black occasion.

Hokey's Roast Potatoes

Serves 2 to 4

From jolly ol' Hokey Dunn, *who loves to cook country food like baked beans and fried mountain oysters, we received this favorite potato recipe. Make them while you're roasting a chicken (page 96) or fixing Auntie's Tender Pork Chops (page 97). I've roasted Hokey's spuds at whatever temperature the oven happens to be offering— 350°F, 400°F, and 425°F. You just have to watch them and adjust the time.*

3   medium Yukon Gold potatoes, scrubbed and quartered, or 1 pound smallish Red Bliss potatoes, scrubbed and halved

¼   cup bottled Italian dressing
½   lemon
     Salt and freshly ground black pepper

Preheat the oven to 400°F.

Line an 8-inch square baking pan with aluminum foil and put the potatoes in it. Combine the dressing and ¼ cup water in a small bowl and pour over the potatoes. Squeeze the lemon over all and sprinkle with salt and pepper to taste. Roast, stirring occasionally, for 45 to 60 minutes, or until the potatoes are tender and browned and all the liquid has been absorbed. Serve hot.

Betty's Quick Coffee Cake

Makes one 8-inch square cake

Could you use a good, *rapid-transit recipe for a coffee-break coffee cake? All aboard for the quintessential crumble-topped cake that got lost in the shuffle of fussy, more glamorous models. Betty Hightower won $25 for the recipe, way back when Bisquick was being introduced. Another reader came up with the orange zest addition, which makes the cake's "Good morning" greeting a little louder.*

2 cups all-purpose baking mix, such as Bisquick	4 tablespoons (½ stick) butter, melted
½ cup sugar	6 tablespoons packed light brown sugar
1 large egg	2 tablespoons all-purpose flour
1 teaspoon grated fresh orange zest	¾ teaspoon ground cinnamon
½ cup orange juice	

Preheat the oven to 400°F. Grease an 8-inch square baking pan. Combine the baking mix, sugar, egg, orange zest, and orange juice in a medium bowl until well blended. Spread in the prepared pan. Combine the butter, brown sugar, flour, and cinnamon in a small bowl and drop by spoonfuls over the batter. Bake

 Note

Don't you love that broom straw, vintage early Bisquick? If you're wall-to-wall-carpeted, substitute a piece of uncooked spaghetti.

for 20 to 25 minutes, or until a tester or broom straw stuck in the center brings up just barely damp crumbs. Do not overbake. Serve warm. The coffee cake reheats well in the microwave.

*I*t was a cold and rainy afternoon. The man stood at the door, holding a foil-covered baking dish. "What's wrong with my coffee cake?" he wanted to know.

Scott Garfield, a debonair octogenarian, had driven down from Brunswick, 35 miles away, to get some answers. He turned back the foil to reveal the remains of Betty's Quick Coffee Cake, a sorry-looking, low-rise affair. At least it was edible. He'd eaten half of it.

While I ran out to retrieve the remains of my own coffee cake from the freezer, Scott pulled up a chair at the table.

My puffy, high-rise specimen only made him more forlorn, but he perked up after I zapped three pieces in the microwave and brought them out with a pot of tea. I suspected his oven and suggested he test it with a new oven thermometer. I also wondered if it was time to replace his box of Bisquick. When teatime was over, I sent him home with what was left of my cake.

A few days later, the Brunswick baker called to report that, sure enough, his oven overheats by 30° at 400°F. He's off to buy a new box of Bisquick. It looks as if there's another Betty's Quick Coffee Cake in his future.

Swedish Grape Pudding (Kram)

Serves 4

Leigh Ann Schwartzkopf *remembered her Swedish grandmother making a simple pudding with grape juice and a thickener and despaired of ever finding the directions for it (sometimes the simpler it is, the harder it is to get it exactly right). Barbara Larsen read Leigh Ann's search in* Cook & Tell *and promptly sent us the very recipe of Leigh Ann's dreams.*

¼ cup sugar
¼ cup cornstarch
2 cups purple grape juice

Whipped cream
Ground cinnamon

Put the sugar, cornstarch, and ¼ cup water in a medium saucepan and stir until smooth. Gradually add the grape juice over medium-high heat, stirring constantly. Reduce the heat to medium-low and cook, stirring constantly, until dark, clear, and thick, 7 to 8 minutes; allow for the fact that the pudding thickens as it cools. Pour into four dessert dishes (glass is nice) and chill. Serve cold with whipped cream and a dusting of cinnamon.

Waffles, 1-2-3

Makes three 7-inch regular (not Belgian) waffles

This is the easy way to make waffles, *when waffling seems the right thing to do and you can't find the favorite family recipe. This one will soon be that favorite.*

1 8-ounce container fruit yogurt, any flavor	1 cup all-purpose baking mix, such as Bisquick
2 large eggs	¼ cup yellow cornmeal
3 tablespoons vegetable oil	

Preheat a waffle iron.
Using an electric mixer, beat the yogurt, eggs, and oil in a medium bowl. Stir in the baking mix and cornmeal by hand. The batter is pleasantly sweetened by the fruity yogurt, but if you want to add a spoonful of sugar, go right ahead. Ladle out one-third of the batter onto the hot waffle iron for each waffle. Cook until the waffle is golden. Serve hot.

Note

The recipe is easily doubled. These are soft, not crisp and dry, waffles. They invite you to eat them, standing up in the kitchen while you bake them, one, two, three.

 # Cantaloupe Ice

Serves 8

With no egg whites or milk *among its ingredients, this fruit ice doesn't qualify as a sherbet, and it's too simple to call a sorbet. But when grades are given for the all-important taste test, this frozen refresher passes with flying colors. You don't even need an ice-cream machine to make it.*

2 cups fresh cantaloupe cubes
(about 1/2 cantaloupe)

1/4 cup sugar

1 12-ounce can ginger ale
(1 1/2 cups)

1/4 cup sweetened lime juice,
such as Rose's

Put the cantaloupe, sugar, 1/2 cup of the ginger ale, and the lime juice in a blender jar, cover, and whir until completely blended. Pour in the remaining 1 cup ginger ale—it should just fit—and stir with a spoon. Pour into 2 aluminum ice-cube trays with the dividers removed, or another shallow pan or dish, and place in the freezer. Stir with a fork after 1 hour, and every so often thereafter (allowing about 3 hours from start to finish), until frozen but "flaky." That's the proper texture for serving, and it should remain that way.

If you're making the ice in advance, pile it lightly into a 1-quart container, cover, and leave it in the freezer for up to 2 weeks. Shortly before serving, remove the ice from the freezer and give it another stir and toss, if necessary.

  Note

You can make the ice in a food processor, but I love my old blender. Lime juice, which you can find in the supermarket, comes in a pretty bottle, already sweetened.

Hot Apple Sundaes

Serves 6

Susan Delaney-Mech, *consulting food chemist to* Cook & Tell *(well, she's a chemist, she likes to cook, and she's a subscriber), dreamed up this topping for glorious autumn sundaes. Ladies and gentlemen, it may sound like just apples and maple syrup, but let me tell you, something wonderful happens in the oven. Call it chemistry. Use only McIntosh apples; they turn properly slurpy in the designated time.*

5 McIntosh apples, peeled, cored, and diced	3 tablespoons pure maple syrup
	1 quart vanilla ice cream

Preheat the oven to 350°F.

Put the diced apples in an 8-inch square baking dish. Stir in the maple syrup. Cover and bake for 1 hour, or until the apples are soft. At serving time, dole out the ice cream into six bowls or sundae dishes. Ladle the hot topping over the ice cream and serve immediately.

· midsummer eve's supper ·

Lobster at Robinson's Wharf

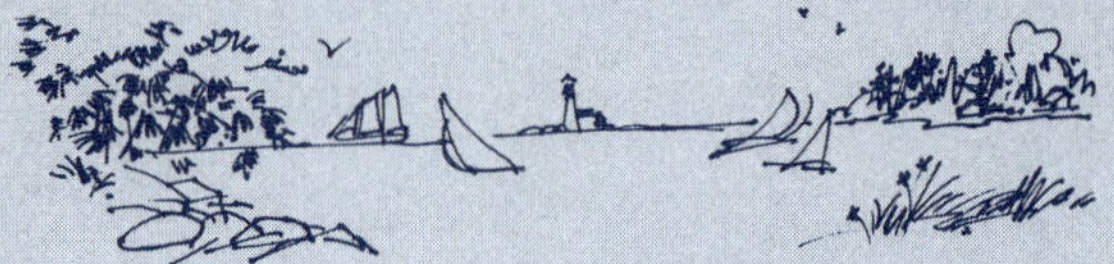

Barefoot buffet at the beach

Saltwater Summer

· Dinner aboard the boat ·

The way
LiFE
should
TASTE

Baked Fish Chowder

Serves 10

It gets cool when the sun goes down *around here, and it can often be cool right in the middle of a beautiful, sunny day, too. Chowder, therefore, is a year-round favorite on Maine tables. Joy Dineen's friend Rachel adds a few surprises to this Maine staple, not the least of which is the fact that you bake it. So when the forecast calls for shorts and bare feet, you can make this in the cool, early morning, when the kitchen could use a warm-up, and heat it up in a kettle or saucepan that night for supper.*

2 pounds haddock, hake, or pollack fillets	1/4 teaspoon chili powder
4 medium potatoes, peeled and cubed	1 garlic clove, crushed
1/2 cup chopped fresh celery leaves	1 bay leaf
2 1/2 teaspoons salt	3 medium onions, cut into chunks
1/4 teaspoon freshly ground black pepper	8 tablespoons (1 stick) butter, cut into 8 pieces
1/4 teaspoon cayenne pepper	1/4 teaspoon dried dill weed
	2 cups half-and-half or light cream

Preheat the oven to 375°F.

Put the fish in a 3-quart casserole dish with a cover or a Dutch oven. Layer the potatoes and celery leaves on top of the fish. Sprinkle with the salt, pepper, cayenne, and chili powder, then add the garlic and bay leaf. Top with the onions, butter, and dill. Pour in 2^1/$_4$ cups boiling water. Cover and bake for 1 hour. Scald the half-and-half or cream and stir it into the chowder. Remove the bay leaf and serve hot with crusty bread or crackers.

Corn and Crab Chowder
with Other Options

Serves 8

If corn chowder is so country-kitchen good *and we all love crabmeat, why don't we just put them together for a bang-up coastal-country potful? This combination features our delicate Maine crab, but any crabmeat works. Have a look at those options. What we have here is customized chowder.*

2	tablespoons (¹⁄₄ stick) butter	
4	bacon slices, cut into ¹⁄₂-inch pieces	
1	large onion, chopped	
2	potatoes, peeled and cubed	
1	1-pound can whole-kernel corn, drained (reserve the liquid)	
1	1-pound can cream-style corn	
2	cups half-and-half, light cream, or milk	

¹⁄₂ teaspoon celery salt
¹⁄₄ teaspoon freshly ground black pepper
6–8 ounces fresh Maine crabmeat (or any other kind)
Options: flaked smoked trout, chopped cooked clams, smoked clams, cubed cooked ham

Melt the butter in a large saucepan over medium heat and sauté the bacon until cooked through; it needn't be crisp. Add the onion and sauté until limp and translucent, about 5 minutes. Add the potatoes, reserved corn liquid, and water to cover. Simmer, partially covered, until the potatoes are cooked through, about 10 minutes. Add

the whole-kernel corn; cream-style corn; half-and-half, light cream, or milk; celery salt; and pepper. Heat through, but do not boil. Just before serving, add the crabmeat and any of the options, if using, and heat through. Serve hot with crusty bread or crackers.

Island Seafood Chowder

Serves 10 to 12

From a Prince Edward Island *craftswoman comes a seafood chowder I call "finest kind," as they say around here in Maine.*

- 2 medium potatoes, peeled and cubed
- 1 pound mussels, debearded and scrubbed
- 2 large onions, chopped
- 1 cup chopped celery
- 2 garlic cloves, minced
- 2 bay leaves
- 1 ¹/₄-pound haddock fillet
- 1 ¹/₄-pound salmon fillet

- ¹/₄ pound scallops
- ¹/₂ pound shrimp, peeled and deveined
- 4 tablespoons (¹/₂ stick) butter
- ¹/₄ cup all-purpose flour
- 1 carrot, peeled and grated
- 4 cups milk
- Salt and freshly ground black pepper

Cook the potatoes in a medium saucepan of boiling water until cooked through, about 10 minutes. Drain and set aside.

Put the mussels, half of the onions, ¹/₂ cup of the celery, garlic, bay leaves, and 1 cup water in a Dutch oven or other large, heavy-bottomed pot over medium-high heat and bring to a boil. Reduce the heat to medium-low and simmer for 5 minutes, or until the mussels open. Remove the mussels and pick out the meat; discard the shells and any unopened mussels. You should have about ³/₄ cup mussels. Strain the stock, discard the solids, and return the stock to the pot over medium-low heat. Add the haddock, salmon, and scallops and simmer until opaque, about 8 minutes. Add the shrimp for the last few minutes of cooking (2 minutes for small Maine shrimp). Strain, set aside the seafood, and reserve the stock. You should have about 2 cups seafood. Rinse out the pot.

Melt the butter in the pot over medium heat and sauté the remaining onions and remaining ¹/₂ cup celery until the onions are limp and translucent, about 5 minutes. Add the flour and cook, stirring, for 1 minute. Add the carrot and whisk in the reserved stock and the milk. Simmer for 15 minutes, or until the carrot is tender. Add the cooked seafood and potatoes. Gently break up the fish as it heats through. Season with salt and pepper to taste. Serve hot with crusty bread or crackers.

*I*t always seems to be a mad-dogs-and-Englishmen kind of day, sun straight up and hot, when the Southport Methodist Church ladies hold their "Christmas in July" luncheon and country fair at the town hall. Barbara, who spends her summers here, and I, who live here year-round, have met there for our annual lobster roll for years.

I always walk to the luncheon at high noon, unencumbered, purseless, my money stashed in what Barbara calls the "Midland Bank," that place protected by one's blouse, just below one's neck, where dollar bills may be safely tucked. This leaves my arms free for swinging and my hands free for picking the roadside wildflowers I can never resist. At least as lovely as chatting with Barbara over lobster rolls is finding a heart-shaped stone along the way, when I stop to shake the gravel out of my sandals.

The ladies have packed our lobster rolls with pure lobster meat mixed with a little mayonnaise and arranged them on paper plates. Potato chips and sour pickle slices are the only accompaniments. Although the beverage table offers a choice, for Barbara and me there is none. What kind of a sunshine-and-lobster-roll luncheon would it be without lemonade?

When our plates are empty, the Methodist men, who ply the narrow aisles between the long tables with their huge dessert trays held aloft, present us with the only challenge of the hour — what to choose from the assortment of homemade cake squares. A refill of lemonade allows us to linger over snapshots of our families and our travels before it is time to go.

Ooh-La-La Lobster Rolls

Serves 4

The traditional lobster roll—*meat from a boiled lobster mixed with nothing but mayonnaise and packed into a toasted hot dog roll—has stood the test of time and simply cannot be improved. Nevertheless, I keep trying. To subdue some of the la-di-da quality of my gussied-up version, I recommend wearing old clothes and sitting on a big rock when you eat them. Or you could forget the rolls and serve the filling as a salad, with more than a few sprigs of watercress.*

$\frac{1}{3}$ cup mayonnaise, plus more if needed

2 large hard-boiled eggs, chopped and finely mashed

3 tablespoons finely chopped roasted red bell pepper (see Note)

2 tablespoons finely chopped sweet pickles

1 tablespoon capers, drained

$\frac{1}{2}$ teaspoon Dijon mustard

$\frac{1}{2}$ teaspoon Old Bay seasoning

$\frac{1}{4}$ teaspoon celery seeds

2–2$\frac{1}{2}$ cups cooked lobster meat, cut into bite-size pieces (see sidebar page 169)

4 Pepperidge Farm Hot & Crusty rolls (3$\frac{1}{2}$ by 2$\frac{1}{2}$ inches) or similar rolls

16 watercress sprigs

To make the dressing: Combine the mayonnaise, eggs, roasted pepper, pickles, capers, mustard, Old Bay seasoning, and celery seeds in a medium bowl. Set aside ¼ cup of the mixture in a cup.

Add the lobster meat to the bowl and mix well. Heat the rolls as directed on the package, split them open (but not all the way through), and pluck out enough of the soft insides to make room for a big scoop of lobster salad. Put a spoonful of the reserved dressing in the bottom of each roll, lay 4 watercress sprigs on each roll, and stuff the rolls with the lobster mixture. Serve immediately.

Note

If you don't roast your own red bell peppers, you can buy them in jars in supermarkets. Choose "roasted bell peppers," not "pimientos."

How to Fix a Lobster

A couple of cooked 1¼-pound lobsters will net you about 2 cups of meat. The best pot to cook them in is an enamelware lobster boiler, one of those enormous white-speckled navy blue jobs with a cover. Pour in water to a depth of about 3 inches (the lobsters needn't be covered with water) and bring to a boil.

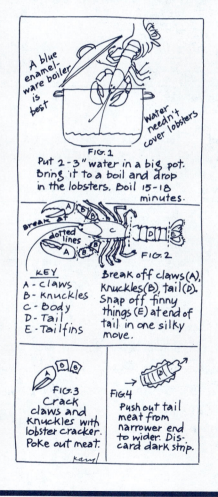

A blue enamelware boiler is best

Water needn't cover lobsters

FIG. 1
Put 2-3" water in a big pot. Bring it to a boil and drop in the lobsters. Boil 15-18 minutes.

Break off dotted lines

FIG. 2

KEY
A - Claws
B - Knuckles
C - Body
D - Tail
E - Tailfins

Break off claws (A), Knuckles (B), tail (D). Snap off finny things (E) at end of tail in one silky move.

FIG. 3
Crack claws and knuckles with lobster cracker. Poke out meat.

FIG. 4
Push out tail meat from narrower end to wider. Discard dark strip.

Plunk the lobsters into the boiling water, cover, and boil for 15 minutes.

Transfer the lobsters to a platter. When cool enough to handle, break off the tails, claws, and knuckles (the knuckles are the parts that connect the big claws to the body). If you're saving the tomalley (the olive-colored stuff in the lobster's fuselage) for another recipe or for a well-deserved private snack after all this work, spoon it out gently. Snap off the finny things at the end of the tail and poke out the meat from the narrow to the wider end of the tail. Pull off and discard the thin, dark strip along the back of the tail meat. Crack the claws with a lobster cracker and poke or pull out the meat. Do the same with the knuckles.

If you feel adventurous, tackle the body: Pull the shell off, gently split the insides down the middle, and "fan out" each side. You'll see little nuggets of meat between the places where those skinny articulated legs attach. Pluck them out and add them to your collection of morsels. There is no such thing as too much lobster meat.

Maine Lobster

Serves 4

Jean Meggison told me *her mother made a heavenly lobster dish, nothing fancy, but so unforgettable that here she was, recalling it practically in living color, over fifty years later.*

When I asked her what they called it, she said her mother just made it and announced, "We're having Maine lobster," as if there was absolutely no other way to serve lobster.

2   tablespoons (¼ stick) butter
2   cups cooked lobster meat, cut into bite-size pieces (see sidebar page 169)
1   cup heavy cream

3–4 cups hot mashed potatoes, seasoned with salt and freshly ground black pepper
Snipped fresh chives (optional)

Melt the butter in a large, heavy-bottomed skillet over medium-low heat and sauté the lobster until the butter picks up its red color, about 5 minutes. Add the cream, increase the heat to medium, and simmer, stirring occasionally, until the cream is reduced by half, about 10 minutes. Divide the mashed potatoes among four warmed bowls. In each serving of potatoes, make a depression with the back of a spoon. Spoon the lobster mixture over the potatoes, making an overflowing lagoon. Snipped chives are a tony garnish that I doubt Jean's mother would have bothered with.

Lobster Stew

Serves 4

Second only to a hot boiled lobster *in the affections of true lobster lovers is a bowl of lobster stew. All you need for the genuine article, the stew that steams out of Maine home kitchens, is this recipe shared by Ellie Hastings, which was given to her by a friend in 1938.*

4 tablespoons (½ stick) butter

2 cups cooked lobster meat, cut into medium chunks (see sidebar page 169)

Salt and freshly ground black pepper

2 cups half-and-half or light cream

2 cups milk

Melt the butter in a medium, heavy-bottomed saucepan over medium-low heat and sauté the lobster until the butter picks up its red color, about 5 minutes. Add ¼ teaspoon each of salt and pepper to start, then the half-and-half or cream and milk. Reduce the heat to low and simmer for 10 to 15 minutes. Adjust the seasonings to taste. The stew tastes best if chilled in the refrigerator for 5 to 6 hours before serving. Reheat over low heat (do not boil) and serve.

 **Note**

Maine folks like to serve lobster stew with Crown Pilot crackers, buttered or plain. They're a famous old cracker available only in stores in New England. But you may order them from Nabisco Customer Service at 1-800-NABISCO, in quantities of 6 or 12 boxes. Common crackers, a substitute most purists would scorn (but they're actually quite good), may be ordered from the Vermont Country Store at 1-802-362-8440.

Little Lobster Casseroles

Serves 4

"Once again our summer was filled with raves for that old COOK & TELL standby, Little Lobster Casseroles. It's the one with tons of butter, crumbs, and chopped pecans. Your recipe called for individual ramekins, but I do it in a shallow casserole with a silly empty lobster shell decorating the top."

— Barbara Bruno

One day down at the lunch place on the coziest harbor in Maine, Marion Bates's mother, Eleanor, shared a lobster reminiscence worth writing down. It turned out to be well worth making and sharing, too. Here's how she remembered a favorite lunch dish from a long-gone Massachusetts restaurant, with some tinkering by me. The quantity of lobster meat depends on how flush you're feeling.

6 tablespoons (³/₄ stick) butter, melted	1 cup finely chopped pecans
3–4 cups cooked lobster meat, cut into bite-size pieces (see sidebar page 169)	Tomalley from 3–4 lobsters, (optional; see sidebar page 169)
1¹/₂ cups corn flakes, crushed with a rolling pin but not pulverized	1 tablespoon Worcestershire sauce

Preheat the oven to 400°F.

Coat the bottoms of four individual-portion ramekins with a small amount of the melted butter. Divide the lobster meat evenly among the ramekins.

To make the topping: Combine the corn flake crumbs, pecans, tomalley (if using), 4 tablespoons of the melted butter, and the

Worcestershire in a medium bowl. Divide the mixture among the ramekins, spreading it lightly over the lobster meat. Drizzle the remaining butter over the crumb mixture. Bake for 15 minutes, or until heated through. Serve hot.

Skillet Fish and Rice

Serves 4

My mother-in-law got a kick out of *cooking in the funky studio apartment she and my father-in-law used to rent in a summer artist colony that perched on pilings over a picturesque harbor. She never knew what utensils she'd find from year to year, what kind of pans, whether there would be a toaster, all spoons and no forks, things like that. The fun was in the surprise, and in the improvising. This uncomplicated dish was invented in that place, using the local fish she found at the fishmonger's and the cast-iron skillet she was fortunate enough to find in the apartment one summer.*

4 bacon slices	1/2 teaspoon salt
1 1/2 cups uncooked white rice (not quick-cooking)	4 flounder or sole fillets
1 1/2 cups bottled clam juice	1 orange, thinly sliced

In a large cast-iron or other heavy skillet, cook the bacon until crisp. Drain and set the bacon aside, reserving 2 tablespoons bacon fat in the skillet. Add the rice and sauté over medium heat for 3 minutes, or until the rice grains are translucent. Add the clam juice, 1 cup water, and the salt. Put the fillets on top, cover, and simmer for 20 minutes, or until the rice is just tender and the fish is cooked through. No need to stir while it's cooking, but it will taste clammier near the bottom of the skillet, so be sure to dig down when serving. Arrange the orange slices around the edge of the skillet, crumble the bacon over the top, and serve from the skillet.

 **Note**

Brown rice was always my mother-in-law's choice. If you use it, cook it in the water and clam juice for about 20 minutes before adding the fish. Then cook for about 20 minutes more, or until the rice is tender.

Haddock Baked Auntie's Way

Serves 6

When I asked Auntie what she likes to do with haddock, she took her recipe notebook off the shelf and went right to the casserole section. "This recipe," she announced with the authority of experience. "This is how I cook it," and she handed me a pencil and a three-by-five file card. She was the original folksy-not-fancy cook, perfectly happy using evaporated milk instead of cream. When you read her recipes, you can tell what the finished product will taste like. And you know it will be delicious.

3 medium potatoes, peeled
   and sliced
1 pound haddock or cusk fillets
1/2 teaspoon salt
1 teaspoon fresh lemon juice

The View from Auntie's Window

White Sauce

2 tablespoons (1/4 stick) butter
2 tablespoons all-purpose flour
1/3 cup evaporated milk
1 teaspoon Worcestershire
   sauce
1/2 teaspoon salt
1/8 teaspoon freshly ground black
   pepper

1 cup soft, fresh bread crumbs
1 tablespoon butter

Cook the sliced potatoes in a medium saucepan of boiling water until barely tender, about 5 minutes. Drain and set aside.

Put the fish in a small saucepan with the salt, lemon juice, and water barely to cover (about 1 cup). Cook until opaque, about 8 minutes. Drain, reserving the stock. Put the fish in a 1^1/$_2$-quart casserole dish or other baking dish and layer the potatoes on top.

Preheat the oven to 375°F.

To make the white sauce: Melt the butter in a small saucepan over medium heat. Add the flour and cook, stirring constantly, for 2 minutes. Add the reserved fish stock, evaporated milk, ^{1}/$_2$ cup water, Worcestershire, salt, and pepper and cook, stirring constantly until thick and smooth, about 4 to 5 minutes.

Pour the sauce over the potatoes. Top with the bread crumbs and dot with the butter. Bake for 30 minutes, or until the fish flakes easily with a fork and the crumbs are golden brown. Serve hot.

Codfish Cakes

Serves 8

We used to have this plain, *old-fashioned, real New England classic with baked beans when I was a kid. It had been so long since I'd made codfish cakes that I'd forgotten all about this great supper dish, until Paula Rougny reminded me with her adaptation of a recipe from one in* Mystic Seaport's Seafood Secrets Cookbook. *I've been making them regularly ever since.*

I proclaim codfish cakes, with Auntie's No-Soak, Cold-Water, White-Sugar Baked Beans (page 188), an eminently appropriate and perfectly excellent Saltwater Summer supper, one that works all year round.

1	1-pound package boned salt cod	2	large eggs, lightly beaten
8	medium potatoes, peeled and cubed	2	tablespoons (¼ stick) butter, melted
1	small onion, minced		Freshly ground black pepper
6	saltine crackers, crushed	2–4	tablespoons vegetable oil
¼	cup chopped fresh parsley		Ketchup or tartar sauce

R inse the salt cod under cold running water for 10 minutes. Put it in a large saucepan, cover with water, and heat slowly, but *do not boil*. Just this side of boiling, pour off the water. Repeat the water-heating step at least two more times, or until the fish no longer tastes salty (it may take a total of four times).

Put the potatoes in a Dutch oven or other large, heavy-bottomed pot and lay the salt cod on top. Add cold water to cover and bring to a boil. Reduce the heat to medium-low and simmer, covered, until the potatoes are tender and the fish flakes with a fork, about 10 minutes. Drain well. Transfer to a large bowl, roughly mash the potatoes by hand, and cool briefly. Stir in the onion, cracker crumbs, parsley, eggs, butter, and pepper to taste. Do not overmix; the texture should be on the rough side.

> **Note**
>
> *These cakes are easily frozen and then defrosted and reheated in the oven or microwave as you need them.*

Cover and chill the mixture for several hours. Form the mixture into cakes about ³/₄ inch thick. Heat 2 tablespoons oil in a large skillet over medium-high heat and fry the cakes in batches for 4 to 5 minutes per side, or until crisp and golden brown. Add more oil if necessary. Serve with ketchup or tartar sauce.

Dishwasher Blues

*M*y favorite guests at my summer house on Martha's Vineyard cook with me and leave behind, as house gifts, their favorite recipes," writes a reader from Boston. "One friend gutted a bluefish we'd caught; left the head and tail on; removed the backbone; stuffed the cavity with bread cubes, celery, ginger, apples, and onion; wrapped the critter in foil; and placed it on the top rack of my dishwasher. We put it through all the cycles. Perfect results! I've done it with salmon, too."

Very Special Tartar Sauce

Makes about 1 cup

The Martha's Vineyard hostess *who cooked bluefish in her dishwasher (see above) claims she's had husbands follow her into the kitchen for this recipe, which the bluefish man gave her when he left. It's a "sensational-looking high riser" of a topping for baked fish fillets.*

Beat 2 large egg whites until stiff but not dry in a medium bowl. Fold in ¼ cup mayonnaise, ¼ cup sweet pickle relish, and 2 tablespoons chopped parsley.

Spread the sauce on fully cooked fish fillets. Pop them under a preheated broiler until browned and bubbly. Serve hot.

Crab Cakes
with Remoulade Sauce

Serves 4; makes about 1 cup sauce

From the café of *Cook & Teller Laura Cabot, where good, casual gourmet food is served, comes Laura's crab cakes, one of the Ladies' Home Journal's "No-Fail Recipes of the Pros." They're easy, quick, and practically ethereal. Make the sauce a day ahead to let the flavors marry.*

Remoulade Sauce

- ½ cup mayonnaise
- 2 tablespoons chopped fresh parsley
- 1 tablespoon Dijon mustard
- 1 tablespoon chopped drained capers
- 1 tablespoon sweet pickle relish
- 1 tablespoon minced fresh tarragon or 1½ teaspoons dried
- 1 teaspoon anchovy paste

Crab Cakes

- 1 pound fresh crabmeat, flaked, or 3 cups cooked salmon, cod, or other fish
- 1 cup soft, fresh bread crumbs
- ¼ cup minced scallions (white and light green parts)
- 3 tablespoons mayonnaise
- 1 large egg, lightly beaten
- 1 teaspoon dry mustard
- 1 teaspoon Worcestershire sauce
- ¼ teaspoon salt
- ¼ teaspoon freshly ground black pepper
- ½ cup plain, dry bread crumbs
- 2-4 tablespoons vegetable oil

To make the sauce: Combine all the ingredients in a small bowl, cover, and chill.

To make the crab cakes: Combine the crabmeat or fish, *fresh* bread crumbs, scallions, mayonnaise, egg, mustard, Worcestershire, salt, and pepper in a medium bowl. Spread the *dry* bread crumbs on a sheet of wax paper. Shape the crab or fish mixture into eight 3-inch-wide cakes. Coat the cakes with the dry bread crumbs.

Heat 1 tablespoon oil in a large nonstick skillet over medium-high heat. (A nonstick electric skillet is swell.) Add four of the cakes and fry for 3 to 4 minutes per side, or until golden. Wipe out the skillet with a paper towel and fry the remaining cakes, adding more oil to the skillet when necessary. Serve hot with the remoulade sauce.

Savory Scallops Baked in Shells

Serves 6

The more you talk *with the best Maine cooks, the more infinite seem the ways with the tasty scallop. Cook them unceremoniously in crumbs or cream, or dress them up in Sunday best, like this. Place smaller portions in more shells and serve them as hors d'oeuvres. Oven-safe scallop shells are available in gourmet shops and kitchen boutiques.*

1½ cups milk	1 celery rib, minced
1 pound scallops	2 tablespoons finely chopped
2 tablespoons (¼ stick) butter	fresh parsley
¾ cup finely chopped lettuce	½ cup fine, dry bread crumbs
¾ cup finely chopped fresh	or cracker crumbs
spinach	2 tablespoons anchovy paste
1 small onion, minced	

Heat the milk in a medium saucepan over medium-high heat until almost boiling. Remove from the heat, add the scallops, and let stand for 10 minutes. Drain and discard the milk.

Meanwhile, melt the butter in a medium skillet over medium heat and sauté the lettuce, spinach, onion, celery, and parsley until softened, about 5 minutes. Stir in the bread crumbs or cracker crumbs and anchovy paste.

Preheat the broiler, with a rack set about 5 inches from the broiling element.

Reserve one-third of the bread-crumb mixture and divide the remainder among six large, oven-safe scallop shells. If the scallops are large, cut them in half. Distribute the scallops evenly among the shells, placing them atop the bread-crumb mixture. Sprinkle the remaining bread-crumb mixture over the scallops. Set the filled shells on a broiler pan and broil for 8 to 10 minutes, or until nicely browned. Serve hot.

 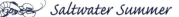

Blue and Bluer Slaw

Serves 6

Inspired by Scandinavian *cabbage-and-fruit combinations, I put this one together and granted it Most Flavored Slaw status. Come on over, and we'll pick all the blueberries we need along the Cape road. And how about adding chopped, unpeeled red apples, for a red, white, and blue Fourth of July salad?*

If you can't get to Maine at blueberry time or can't find blueberries at your local market or fruit stand, increase the grapes to 2 cups.

3 cups shredded cabbage	**Dressing**
1½ cups purple grapes	6 tablespoons mayonnaise
1 11-ounce can mandarin oranges, drained (reserve the juice)	2 tablespoons sugar
	2 teaspoons reserved mandarin orange juice
½ cup fresh blueberries	½ cup crumbled blue cheese (about 2 ounces)
	½ cup walnut halves, toasted

Combine the cabbage, grapes, mandarin oranges, and blueberries in a large bowl.

To make the dressing: Combine the mayonnaise and sugar in a small bowl. Thin the dressing with the reserved orange juice, using more if you'd like it thinner. Stir in the blue cheese.

Pour the dressing over the salad and toss well. Add the walnuts just before serving.

Note

If you have a good chef's knife and know how to use it, slice the cabbage razor thin instead of shredding it.

Summer Corn Casserole

Serves 6

Oh, corn! Oh, tomatoes! *They're the very definition of summer, and when they're layered in a casserole like this one from Jean Lester, it feels like summer will never end. "This recipe sounds very simple," says Jean, and she's right, "but it tastes so complex," and she's right again. We think it's just as good, if not better, reheated. And reheated again.*

4 teaspoons butter	2 teaspoons chopped fresh basil
¼ cup all-purpose flour	Kernels from 4 ears uncooked corn
¾ teaspoon salt	2 medium onions or 1 Vidalia or other sweet onion, thinly sliced
¾ teaspoon freshly ground black pepper	
3 large tomatoes, cut into ½-inch-thick slices	3 slices good-quality white sandwich bread
2 tablespoons olive oil	
1 garlic clove, halved	

Preheat the oven to 325°F. Butter a 2-quart casserole dish with 1 teaspoon of the butter.

Combine the flour, ¼ teaspoon of the salt, and ¼ teaspoon of the pepper on a plate and dredge the tomato slices in the mixture. Heat the oil in a large skillet over medium heat and sauté the garlic until it begins to smell good, about 1 minute; discard the garlic. Sauté the tomato slices in the same oil for 3 minutes per side, or until beginning to soften. Place half of the tomato slices in the prepared dish. Sprinkle with 1 teaspoon of the basil. Add a layer of half the corn and half the onions. Sprinkle ¼ teaspoon of the salt and ¼ teaspoon of the pepper over all. Repeat the layers, using the remaining corn, onions, 1 teaspoon basil, ¼ teaspoon salt, and ¼ teaspoon pepper. Butter the bread slices with the remaining 3 teaspoons butter, stack the slices, and cut them into teeny cubes. Spread the bread cubes over the top of the casserole. Bake for 35 to 45 minutes, or until bubbly and browned. Serve hot.

Auntie's No-Soak, Cold-Water, White-Sugar Baked Beans

Serves 8

A foggy day on the coast of Maine *is made for baking beans. None are as flavorful, as perfectly seasoned, as beautifully brown as Auntie's.*

You should probably be home the whole time they're baking, so you'll be on hand to add water every so often. If you slip out for an hour and come back to beans with their tongues hanging out for thirst, don't blame me. Freeze them and trot them out later for barbecues, patio buffets, and clambakes when it's too hot to bake.

1 pound small white beans (**not** pea beans)	½ teaspoon freshly ground black pepper
¼ pound salt pork	Dab of prepared mustard (any kind)
½ cup white sugar	¼–⅓ cup molasses
1 tablespoon salt	

Preheat the oven to 350°F.

Chuck everything but the molasses into a 2- or 3-quart bean pot. Add cold water to cover the beans. Cover and bake for about 1 hour, or until the beans are plumpish and the skins somewhat shriveled. Add the molasses, reduce the oven temperature to 300°F, cover, and bake until the beans are thoroughly tender, about 6 hours. You'll need to add water just about every hour. The beans must *not* go dry on top. That's an order. Serve hot.

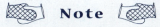 **Note**

Auntie gives it to you straight: Baked beans made in a Crock-Pot or pressure cooker are not baked beans. Baked beans are baked in the place where things bake, the oven. You put them in an old-fashioned bean pot with a handle on one side, and you bake them until they're done. I asked her, "Is that about six hours?" Auntie, who punched a time clock when she worked at the Iron Works in Bath, Maine, during World War II and claimed she had it on good authority that Boston baked beans originated in Maine, said she doesn't count hours. "They're in by ten, out by five."

THE Cold Baked Bean Sandwich

I *grew up on baked bean sandwiches. Savory with a touch* of sweet, full-flavored, friendly to the tooth, bumpy and smooth, rustic yet sophisticated.

Home-baked beans on Saturday nights were all well and good—and Mummy's beans were good—but what made them so good was the promise they held, not just of leftovers reheated and served on a plate, but of leftovers cold, mixed with mayonnaise and chopped onion and laid between two pieces of bread.

There are no fixed quantities to this delicacy, which I still endorse enthusiastically. Mash at least some of the beans—not all, now—with a fork, before mixing with the mayonnaise and onion. Use whole wheat bread and no lettuce.

Blueberry Gelatin Ring

Serves 8 at a Ladies' Luncheon; 6 at home

Everybody's invited to the *Ladies' Luncheons at the yacht club—even the men, if they dare. The clubhouse, overlooking Cozy Harbor, is one of the oldest houses on the island, a wonderful cape built around 1760.*

If you bring a casserole, a salad, or a dessert, there's no charge. If you don't, you pay the tremendous fee of $5.00 for a splendid buffet lunch that might include this salad. I did a little ad-libbing with Flo Woods's recipe and came up with something I think both natives and "summercators" will love. It'll be up to each one to decide whether to call it salad or dessert.

EVERYONE'S INVITED TO
The Yacht Club Luncheon

2½ cups fresh blueberries
1 3-ounce package blackberry
   gelatin
1 3-ounce package raspberry
   gelatin

1 20-ounce can crushed pineapple, with its juice
2 cups cubed watermelon

Cream-Cheese Topping
(recipe follows)

Put 2 cups of the blueberries and 1½ cups water in a medium saucepan and bring to a boil. Remove from the heat and add both gelatins, stirring until completely dissolved. Stir in the pineapple. Pour into a wet 2-quart ring mold and chill until fully set. Turn out the mold onto a platter and surround it with the watermelon cubes and the remaining ½ cup blueberries. Serve with the Cream-Cheese Topping on the side.

Cream-Cheese Topping

1   8-ounce package cream cheese, softened
1   cup sour cream
¼   cup confectioners' sugar

Thoroughly mix the cream cheese and sour cream in a medium bowl. Add the confectioners' sugar and mix well.

Rakin' the BLUES

Joanie B.'s Blueberry Muffins

Makes 12 muffins

These eggless blueberry beauties *have a light, moist crumb that beats out the cakelike competition. Frozen blueberries also perform admirably here, and there's no fussing about tossing the berries with some of the flour, either; you just fold them in and let them fall where they may.*

2 cups all-purpose flour

1 cup plus 2 teaspoons sugar

4 teaspoons baking powder

1 cup milk

3 tablespoons butter, melted

1 cup fresh blueberries (unthawed frozen berries are fine)

Preheat the oven to 350°F. Line a 12-cup muffin tin with paper liners.

Combine the flour, 1 cup sugar, and baking powder in a medium bowl. Stir in the milk—no electric mixer, please—and add the melted butter. Fold in the blueberries. Spoon the batter into the paper-lined muffin tin, filling each cup about two-thirds full. Sprinkle with the remaining 2 teaspoons sugar. Bake for 25 minutes, or until a cake tester stuck in the center of a muffin comes out clean. (Frozen berries don't take extra time here.) Let cool in the tin on a rack for 10 minutes before removing the muffins from the tin. Serve warm or at room temperature.

The Pastor's Blueberry Pie

Serves 6

The Reverend David Stinson *of the Congregational Church in the Harbor helps his church raise money by contributing home-made pies for its auctions. Thinking his recipe deserved to be immortalized, David prayed I might publish it in* Cook & Tell. *Blessed is the man who invents a great blueberry pie and shares the recipe!*

Reverend Stinson's grandfather believed that it was a sin to cut a pie into more than six pieces. So we always cut David's blueberry pie into sixths and fervently eat the whole thing. And, behold, it is very good.

1 cup plus 1 tablespoon sugar
¼ cup all-purpose flour
  Grated zest of ½ lemon
  Juice of ½ lemon
1 large egg
4 cups fresh blueberries (un-thawed frozen berries are fine)

Pastry for a double-crust 9-inch pie (see Fail-Safe Piecrust, page 311)
2 tablespoons milk

Preheat the oven to 450°F.
Combine the 1 cup sugar, flour, lemon zest, lemon juice, and egg in a large bowl. Stir in the blueberries. Roll out half of the pastry and

line a pie plate. Trim, leaving a ¹/₂-inch overhang. Fill with the blue-berry mixture. Roll out the top crust, cut vents, and fit it on the pie. Seal and crimp the edges. Brush the top crust with the milk and sprin-kle with the remaining 1 tablespoon sugar. Bake for 10 minutes. Re-duce the oven temperature to 350°F and bake for 40 minutes more, or until the filling is bubbling and the crust is golden brown. (Add about 20 minutes for frozen berries.) Serve warm or at room temperature.

Note

I make a peek-through lattice as a nice alternative for the top crust.

Blueberry Pecan Pie

Serves 8

"Surrealistic!"

— Don Cavanaugh

What a pie! *I had to bake it twice before I had this hybrid right. I like the nuts chopped, so they're not hard to plow through with a knife or fork, but you can use pecan halves, if you like. Blueberries and a hint of lemon add summery highlights to a rich dessert that cries out for a whipped cream garnish.*

1   cup packed dark brown sugar
1   cup dark corn syrup
3   large eggs, lightly beaten
1/3   cup butter, melted
1   teaspoon grated fresh lemon zest
1   teaspoon fresh lemon juice
1   teaspoon vanilla extract
1/2   teaspoon salt
1   cup fresh blueberries (un-thawed frozen berries are fine)
    Pastry for a single-crust 9-inch pie (see Fail-Safe Piecrust, page 311)
1¼   cups chopped pecans
    Whipped cream, for garnish

Preheat the oven to 350°F.
Using an electric mixer, thoroughly combine the brown sugar, corn syrup, eggs, butter, lemon zest, lemon juice, vanilla, and salt in a large bowl. Fold in the blueberries.

Roll out the pastry and line a pie plate. Trim, leaving a 1-inch over-hang. Fold and crimp the overhang. Pour the blueberry mixture into the crust and sprinkle the pecans over the top. Bake for 45 to 55 minutes, or until the top begins to crack and the juice bubbles around the edge. (Add 15 to 20 minutes for frozen berries.) Serve cold for best slicing, with a garnish of whipped cream.

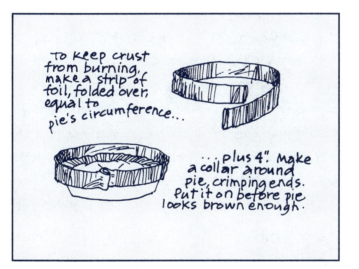

To keep crust from burning, make a strip of foil, folded over, equal to pie's circumference...

...plus 4". Make a collar around pie, crimping ends. Put it on before pie looks brown enough.

Eleanor's 1921 Lemon Sherbet with Hot Blueberry Sauce

Makes 1 gallon

*"I made the Hot Blueberry Sauce and poured it over a bowl of buttered white bread cut into triangles. I covered it with plastic wrap and let it stand overnight. This recipe is from my stepmother (with COOK & TELL's sauce patched in), who was not much of a cook, **but who tried!** It's the only recipe I ever called up to ask her about. She was terribly flattered."*

— Judith Woodbury

From this dainty and dear *lady came many of my favorite old recipes, ones she made over and over again through the years of her long life. Packing her recipes along with her summer clothes, she came to her coastal cottage in Maine for over sixty seasons.*

This is no watery sorbet or icy granita. This is what sherbet used to be. After the old hand-cranked ice-cream freezers gave way to the new electric ones, Eleanor made her sherbet with a freezer that used ice cubes and table salt. I use one with a gel-filled cylinder that stays in the freezer until you're ready to use it. Neither contraption holds the whole recipe, so we make half, and that's sometimes just enough. The blueberry sauce is Betty Marshall's favorite lemon sherbet topper.

1¼	cups fresh lemon juice (about 3 lemons)	8 cups (2 quarts) milk
3	cups sugar	2 cups heavy cream
⅛	teaspoon salt	Hot Blueberry Sauce (recipe follows)

Combine the lemon juice, sugar, and salt in a medium bowl. Combine the milk and cream in a large bowl and add the sugar mix-

ture. Stir until the sugar is dissolved. No cooking! Freeze in batches in an ice-cream freezer, according to the manufacturer's instructions. Serve with Hot Blueberry Sauce. The sherbet keeps, tightly covered, in the freezer for up to 1 week.

Hot Blueberry Sauce

Makes about 1 cup

1½ cups fresh blueberries (un-
    thawed frozen berries are
    fine)
¼ cup sugar
¾ teaspoon ground cinnamon

½ teaspoon grated fresh lemon
    zest
¼ teaspoon ground nutmeg
1 tablespoon finely chopped
    crystallized ginger

Combine the blueberries, sugar, cinnamon, lemon zest, and nutmeg in a small saucepan over medium-high heat and bring to a boil. You don't need any water; the berries provide enough liquid. Reduce the heat to low and simmer for 5 minutes, stirring occasionally. Remove from the heat and stir in the ginger. Serve hot.

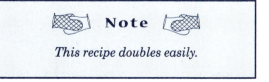 **Note**

This recipe doubles easily.

## Chapter 7

Honk if you love veggies

Garden of Eating

The Search for Roots

Hooray for produce

Eat your vegetables

Scallions and Peas

Serves 4

After winter surrenders *to spring's forward March, we all want our vegetables to be as green as possible. To celebrate the victory of spring, we invite scallions, aka green onions, for dinner, along with ever-popular green peas. Join us for a great moment of greenness!*

4 bunches scallions, nasty ends trimmed but with lots of green left	¹⁄₂ teaspoon salt
	Pinch of sugar
	2 cups frozen baby peas

Cut the trimmed scallions into 1¹⁄₂-inch lengths, separating the white and green parts. Put the white scallion pieces, salt, and sugar in a medium saucepan with ¹⁄₂ inch of boiling water. Simmer over medium-low heat, covered, for 2 minutes. Add the green scallion pieces, increase the heat to medium, and simmer for 3 minutes more, or until almost tender. Add the peas and cook until heated through, about 3 minutes more. Serve hot.

Angie's Cold Broccoli

Serves 4 to 6

Must a cooked vegetable side dish *always be served hot? Time's up. Time to cook broccoli and serve it Angie's way, not warm, not at room temperature either, but as cold as Greenland's icy mountains. Alice Peters, who'd rather send recipes than cook, wrote, "My friend Ann says this is delicious, as green as green can be. Angie is Italian, so it must be good." It certainly deserves* Cook & Tell's *AAA rating, and not just because it passed from Angie to Ann to Alice.*

1¹⁄₂–2 pounds broccoli stalks	Freshly ground black pepper
Salt	¹⁄₂–1 lemon
6 garlic cloves	3 tablespoons olive oil

Trim the woody ends of the broccoli stalks and peel away the tough outer layer.

Put the broccoli in a medium saucepan with 2¹⁄₂ inches of boiling, salted water. Simmer over medium heat for 5 minutes, or until barely tender. Drain, plunge the broccoli into cold water to stop the cooking, and drain again. Cool to room temperature. Arrange the broccoli on a platter. Using a garlic press, press the garlic over the broccoli, distributing it evenly. Sprinkle with salt and pepper to taste, then squeeze half a lemon over the broccoli. Use the other half if you really like lemon. Drizzle with the olive oil. Chill until serving time. Serve cold.

Asparagus ASAP

Serves 4

For this dish you need *one of those deep-frying baskets, plus a bit of skill with a chef's knife. And you thought the only way to cook asparagus was standing them up in an asparagus steamer or simmering them in a reclining position, in an inch of water in a skillet.*

1 pound asparagus
Salt

slice asparagus obliquely on the diagonal

Final Flourishes

Melted butter, salt, and freshly ground black pepper
Soy sauce and toasted sesame seeds
Parmesan cheese, grated

Snap off and discard the woody ends of the asparagus stalks. Wash the stalks and peel off the scales with a vegetable peeler or a small, sharp knife. Cut the asparagus on an acute diagonal into exceedingly thin slices whose length is much greater than their width. Put the asparagus slices in a deep-frying basket.

Put the basket of asparagus in a large saucepan one-third full of boiling, salted water. Simmer for 2 minutes, or until crisp-tender. Drain. Serve hot with melted butter, salt, and pepper to taste; soy sauce and toasted sesame seeds; or Parmesan cheese.

Ratatouille

Serves 6

There are classic recipes for this *French country dish, and they're exquisite and complex. But lately I've noticed restaurants offering their versions, as simple as mine, and calling it "Zucchini, Eggplant, and Tomato," which makes it sound as uncomplicated as it is.*

1 medium eggplant
1 medium zucchini
1 large green bell pepper
1 medium onion
¼ cup olive oil, plus more if needed
2 garlic cloves, slivered
1 teaspoon dried thyme

1 teaspoon dried basil
1 teaspoon dried oregano
  Salt and freshly ground black pepper
2 large tomatoes, chopped
2 tablespoons chopped fresh parsley

Cut the eggplant, zucchini, bell pepper, and onion into chunks, slices, or cubes — whatever you feel like tossing around in a skillet. Keep the skin on the eggplant; it's edible and interesting.

Heat the oil in a large skillet over medium heat and add the cut-up vegetables, garlic, thyme, basil, oregano, and salt and pepper to taste. Cover and cook, stirring often, until the vegetables are limp but browned, about 8 minutes. Eggplant has a tremendous capacity to drink up oil; add more if necessary. Add the tomatoes and parsley, increase the heat to medium-high, and cook until the juices are thickened, about 5 minutes. Serve hot.

Tomato and Cheese Pie

Serves 6 to 8

Rita McDonough recommended *this recipe, in which cheese and bacon, in cahoots with eggs and lots of bread crumbs, turn garden tomatoes and onions into a savory pie. Scrimp not on those bread crumbs; use the full allotment. They become a super substitute for a standard piecrust, sopping up juices along the way.*

2 cups soft, fresh bread crumbs
3 large tomatoes, thinly sliced
1 medium onion, thinly sliced
2 cups grated cheddar cheese
   (about 8 ounces)

3 bacon slices, cooked crisp
   and crumbled, plus 3 slices,
   uncooked
2 large eggs
½ teaspoon salt
⅛ teaspoon freshly ground
   black pepper

Preheat the oven to 350°F.
   Cover the bottom of a 10-inch pie plate with 1 cup of the bread crumbs. Layer the tomato slices over the crumbs, followed by the onion slices, then the cheese, and finally the cooked bacon. Beat the eggs, salt, and pepper in a small bowl and pour over the pie. Top with the remaining 1 cup bread crumbs and the uncooked bacon. Bake for

35 to 45 minutes, or until the pie is bubbly and the bacon on top is cooked. Once Rita used a Pyrex dish, and it took 50 minutes. Serve hot.

Tip

From Chef Gus: Tired of losing the juicy innards of a tomato when slicing it horizontally, crosswise, east-and-west? Get to the bottom of the problem by starting at the top and slicing vertically, North Pole to South Pole. Less flesh is wasted, too, since you can get closer to that stemmy place at the top.

Sparkly Cherry Tomatoes

Serves 4

A quick sauté *of ripe, sweet cherry tomatoes is fun to make while a tenderloin roasts in the oven or fish cooks outdoors on the grill. Fix them at the last minute to ensure perfect roundness. The glistening, sweet, red baubles imitate tree ornaments at Christmastime.*

2	tablespoons olive oil	Pinch of sugar
24	cherry tomatoes	Chopped fresh parsley
1	garlic clove, minced	

Heat the oil in a medium skillet over medium-high heat and sauté the tomatoes and garlic until the tomatoes are heated through, about 3 minutes, rolling them around to coat them with oil and garlic bits. Add the sugar, toss, and remove from the heat before the tomatoes collapse. Garnish with a drift of parsley and serve.

Low-Tech Tip

Marietta Witt's indispensable gadget for the unplugged kitchen is an ordinary pair of scissors. "Not *kitchen* scissors," says Marietta, "just scissors, the orange-handled Fiskars scissors I've been using for years. They stay sharp no matter what I cut with them — pizza, bacon, prunes, apricots, spinach, scallions." Here's the Witty way to cut parsley: "Fill a juice glass with washed and dried parsley, stick in the scissors, and cut until it's as fine as you want."

Full-Color Fried Corn

Serves 4

For COOK & TELL's February issue *one year, I concocted this tasty tribute to our beloved presidents, Abe and George. It's a colorful mingling of flavors. A more perfect union would be hard to find.*

2 tablespoons dried cranberries

2 tablespoons olive oil

2 carrots, peeled and thinly sliced or cut into matchsticks

⅓ cup chopped green bell pepper

½ teaspoon chili powder, or more to taste

½ teaspoon ground cumin, or more to taste

Salt and freshly ground black pepper

1 cup unthawed frozen corn

Let the cranberries soak in hot water to cover in a small bowl for 8 minutes, or until softened.

Meanwhile, heat the oil in a large skillet over medium heat and sauté the carrots and bell pepper until limp, about 5 minutes. Stir in the chili powder, cumin, and salt and pepper to taste. Add the corn, stirring to coat with the oil. Cook, stirring, for 3 minutes, or until the corn is heated through. Drain the cranberries, add to the corn mixture, and serve.

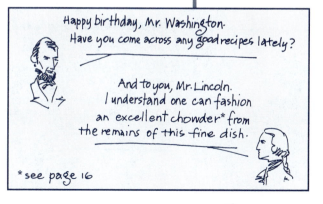

Happy birthday, Mr. Washington. Have you come across any good recipes lately?

And to you, Mr. Lincoln. I understand one can fashion an excellent chowder* from the remains of this fine dish.

*see page 16

Braised Celery and Carrot

Serves 4

Poor, unsung celery is usually *a raw munchy or a mere ingredient, not the main event on a menu. Here, it steps right up and takes a bow for excellence in a leading role. The traditional Irish dish that inspired me, from* Real Irish Cookery *by Mary Caherty, has no carrots. I put them in to round out this folksy recipe.*

1 celery heart with leaves, cut into 1-inch lengths	1 teaspoon chopped fresh parsley
1 medium carrot, peeled and cut into matchsticks	1 cup homemade chicken stock or canned chicken broth
2 bacon slices, partially cooked (not crisp) and finely chopped	Salt and freshly ground black pepper
1 medium onion, finely chopped	2 tablespoons (¼ stick) butter

Preheat the oven to 350°F.
Put the celery and carrot in a 1-quart casserole dish. Strew the chopped bacon over the vegetables, add the onion and parsley, and pour in the stock or broth. Sprinkle with salt and pepper to taste and dot with the butter. Cover and bake for 45 minutes, or until tender. Serve hot.

Sautéed Carrots and Parsnips

Serves 6

These two are splendid characters, *both of them sweet and earthy, but quite different. When cooked, the softer parsnip cozies up to the tender but firm carrot. Sage is the mysterious stranger in this story, turning the dowdy into something worth gossiping about.*

2 tablespoons vegetable oil	3 teaspoons chopped fresh sage
2 tablespoons (¼ stick) butter	½ teaspoon salt
8 carrots, peeled and cut into ¼-inch-thick slices	Freshly ground black pepper
8 parsnips, peeled and cut into ¼-inch-thick slices (see Note)	

Heat the oil and 1 tablespoon of the butter in a large skillet over medium heat. Add the carrots, partially cover, and let them sweat, stirring occasionally, for 4 minutes, or until limp. Add the remaining 1 tablespoon butter, the parsnips, 2 teaspoons of the sage, and the salt. Partially cover and cook for 4 minutes more, stirring occasionally, reducing the heat to avoid scorching, if necessary. Add ½ cup water, cover, and simmer until the vegetables are just tender and all the water has been absorbed, about 4 minutes more, adjusting the temperature if necessary. Sprinkle with lots of pepper, garnish with the remaining 1 teaspoon sage, and serve.

Note

Parsnips are often fat at the top and taper down to skinny at the bottom. Here's how to prepare parsnips with that profile: Cut them crosswise in half where they stop being fat and start getting skinny. Slice the skinny end pieces into 1-inch-thick lengths. Cut the fat pieces vertically into quarters, cut out and discard the woody centers, and slice the pieces crosswise ¼ inch thick.

Glazed Carrots

Serves 4 to 6

As kids, we pulled baby carrots *out of the garden and rubbed them in the grass to clean them. Then we sat on the ground and ate them. And didn't we do the same darned thing when we were all grown up! What do you bet carrots are the one vegetable you'll find in the refrigerator drawers of nine out of ten people? Dress them up with a glaze like this, and you'll win over that tenth person easily.*

6 large carrots, peeled and cut on the diagonal into ½-inch-thick slices	Pinch of salt
	½ cup orange juice or water
	Squirt of fresh lemon juice
4 tablespoons (½ stick) butter	5 scallions (white and light green
2 tablespoons sugar	parts), chopped, for garnish

Put the carrots, butter, sugar, salt, orange juice or water, and lemon juice in a large, heavy skillet and bring to a boil. Reduce the heat to medium-low and cook, covered, for 5 minutes, or until a fork poked into a carrot slice meets with just a bit of resistance. Uncover and cook, stirring often, for 3 minutes more, or until the carrots are just tender and nicely glazed. Transfer to a serving bowl, garnish with the scallions, and serve.

Two-Tone
Mashed Potatoes
with Goat Cheese

Serves 4

These chic mashed potatoes *were a desperate substitute for a recipe that blew up on me, and now I'm glad it did. Sweet potatoes disguised like this will fool even skeptics. If you make this dish in advance, you can freeze it in a baking dish, defrost it, tuck another blob of goat cheese in a depression in the top (so you should have more goat cheese on hand), and reheat it in the oven or microwave.*

2 large Yukon Gold or other baking potato, peeled and cut into ¼-inch-thick slices

1 large-to-humongous sweet potato, peeled and cut into ¼-inch-thick slices

Salt

½ cup half-and-half or heavy cream

1 tablespoon chopped fresh parsley

1 teaspoon chopped fresh rosemary

2 ounces soft goat cheese (with or without herbs) or Boursin cheese

Freshly ground black pepper

Cook the baking potatoes and sweet potato in a large saucepan of boiling, salted water until barely tender, 15 to 20 minutes. Drain and return to the saucepan. Cover and set aside; keep warm.

Meanwhile, heat the half-and-half or cream, parsley, and rosemary in a small saucepan over medium heat until hot but not boiling. Add the cream mixture and the goat cheese to the potatoes and mash with a potato masher for a rustic effect. Add salt and pepper to taste (use plenty of pepper). Serve immediately; keep warm in the top of a double boiler; or freeze, thaw, and reheat in a 350°F oven, as explained in the headnote.

Cheesy Mashed Potato Casserole

Serves 4

What we have here is almost a soufflé, *without the fear of falling. Betty McCreary sent the recipe with a warning: "My recipes are workable only if not tampered with." That's all it takes to scare me into total submission, even with nobody looking. You can prepare this casserole a day or two in advance and keep it in the fridge before baking.*

	Butter	1	heaping cup hot mashed
1	large egg		potatoes
8	ounces cream cheese (not	⅓	cup finely chopped onion
	whipped), softened		Paprika

Preheat the oven to 350°F. Butter a 1-quart baking dish.
Beat the egg lightly with a fork in a medium bowl. Add the cream cheese and blend until smooth. Mix in the mashed potatoes and onion. Transfer to the prepared dish; do not smooth the top. Sprinkle with paprika. Bake for 45 minutes, or until the top has golden brown peaks and ridges. Serve hot.

Squabbage

Serves 6

This improbable combination *was a whim that paid off. Butternut squash loves butter, and cabbage turns tame in the company of both. When you're planning a vegetarian meal and you're in the market for something substantial, colorful, and texturally interesting to accompany brown rice and black beans, for instance, put a squash and a cabbage on your shopping list.*

We ♡ veggies!

4 tablespoons (½ stick) butter	2 cups coarsely chopped cabbage
1 medium butternut squash, peeled, seeded, and cut into 1-inch cubes; or three-fourths 20-ounce package frozen butternut squash pieces, thawed and cut into 1-inch cubes	1 teaspoon salt
	1 teaspoon dried dill weed
	Chopped fresh parsley, for garnish

Melt the butter in a large skillet over medium heat and sauté the squash for 2 minutes. Reduce the heat to medium-low, cover, and simmer, stirring occasionally, for 8 minutes, or until the squash is almost tender. You shouldn't need to add water if the temperature is right, but if you're worried, add up to ½ cup water at any time in the process. Add the cabbage, salt, and dill and toss gently. Simmer, covered, for 5 minutes more, or until the cabbage is barely tender and the squash is soft. Garnish with chopped parsley and serve.

Red Cabbage
with White Grape Juice

Serves 6

The inn at the end of our island *used to serve a good red cabbage dish that was worth reproducing. So I went to work on a clone, finely tuning a subscriber's recipe with zesty updates. Since I had white grape juice on hand, I sent it in as a substitute for water. Now I had a red cabbage dish that was better than the inn's. The balsamic vinegar sets it loose from its traditional German roots. Serve with Fruit Juice–Basted Ham (page 248) and Cheesy Mashed Potato Casserole (page 216).*

1 medium red cabbage, finely shredded (about 8 cups)

2 apples (Cortland, Empire, and Granny Smith are good choices), peeled, cored, and chopped

4 whole cloves

1 teaspoon salt

1 cup white grape juice or 1 cup water + 3 tablespoons sugar

4 tablespoons (¼ stick) butter

2 tablespoons red currant jelly

1 tablespoon balsamic vinegar

¼ teaspoon cayenne pepper

Put the cabbage, apples, cloves, salt, and grape juice or sugar water in a large, nonreactive skillet, such as stainless steel or enameled cast-iron, over medium heat. Simmer, covered, until the cabbage is tender, about 45 minutes. Discard the cloves and stir in the butter, jelly, vinegar, and cayenne. Heat, stirring, until the butter and jelly are melted and well distributed. Serve hot.

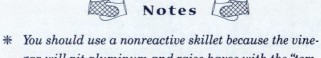

Notes

* *You should use a nonreactive skillet because the vinegar will pit aluminum and raise havoc with the "tempering" of a well-tempered cast-iron skillet.*
* *For a simple but equally tasty sauerkraut dish, Susan Delaney-Mech likes to simmer slightly drained sauerkraut in apple juice.*

Rutabaga and Apple Hash

Serves 6

An unusual-sounding vegetable hash *from Victor Rosasco, former chef at Sorvino's restaurant, prompted me to call him in New York and boldly ask him how to make it. I groaned when he started getting cheffy on me, with his fancy talk about caramelizing bones and mirepoixing vegetables for a reduction he uses for the sauce. So Chef Victor graciously, and not one bit condescendingly, offered the canned-gravy alternative.*

8 tablespoons (1 stick) butter
1 red onion, thinly sliced
1/3 cup packed light brown sugar
1 medium rutabaga, peeled and shredded

1 medium McIntosh or Cortland apple, peeled, cored, and shredded
Salt and freshly ground black pepper
Brown Gravy Sauce (recipe follows)

Melt the butter in a large skillet over medium heat and sauté the onion until limp and translucent, about 5 minutes. Stir in the brown sugar. Add the rutabaga and apple, increase the heat to high, and sauté for 5 minutes more, or until tender. Season with salt and pepper to taste. Serve hot with Brown Gravy Sauce.

Brown Gravy Sauce

Makes about 2 cups

1　14.75-ounce can beef gravy
1　14.5-ounce can chicken broth

Combine the gravy and broth in a saucepan over medium-high heat and simmer until the mixture is reduced by about one-third ("to a nice thickness," said Victor).

Chapter 8

company coming **HAPPY BIRTHDAY**

Party Time Glad Tidings, Good Tastings

The Turkey Tradition ◇ OPEN HOUSE

Best Wishes, Best Dishes

Christmas Comforts mazel tov!

Starters

Anchovy Olives   225

Chicken Liver Pâté   226

Russian Mushroom Caviar   228

Tuscany Toast   229

Party Cheese Crackers   230

Randy's Mushroom Tart   232

Cream Cheese and Hot Pepper Jelly Tart   234

Turkish Boereks   235

Christmas Eve Oyster Stew   237

Cold Curried Shrimp Salad with Chutney Aspic   238

Main Dishes

Crab Imperial for Commoners   240

Turkey Roasted with Whole Fruit and Hot Sausage Stuffing   242

Cranberry-Glazed Pork Roast   246

Fruit Juice–Basted Ham   248

Pepper-Crusted Filet Mignon   250

Roast Tenderloin of Beef with Horseradish Cream   252

Simple Shepherd's Pie for Christmas Eve   254

Tourtière (French-Canadian Meat Pie)   256

Side Dishes

Raspberry Green Beans   258

Roast Chrysanthemum Onions   260

Anchovy Olives

Makes about 1 cup

This recipe makes a tasty tidbit *for a party. It's not tricky or complicated, and it doesn't require a big investment of patience or time. You just have a lot of little pieces here, some to be stuffed with others, that add up to a collection of things that look like jewels and taste like something dreamed up by the chef at the Ritz. You can bet he'd roast his own red bell pepper. That's why he's a chef and we're not.*

1 2-ounce tin flat anchovy
   fillets, drained
1 6-ounce can large, pitted
   black olives, drained
6 tablespoons olive oil
2 tablespoons fresh lemon juice

¼ teaspoon freshly ground
   black pepper
Pinch of salt
1 2-ounce jar sliced pimientos,
   drained
1 garlic clove, halved

Cut the anchovies into ½-to-¾-inch pieces and poke a piece into each olive. Combine the oil, lemon juice, pepper, and salt in a jar, screw on the lid, and shake to blend. Put the stuffed olives and pimientos in a shallow serving bowl and pour the marinade over them. Toss in the garlic. Provide toothpicks for spearing the olives and pimientos.

Chicken Liver Pâté

Makes about 3 cups

Just making this classy, classic spread *is as much fun as a party. But when you're all done, there you are with more than enough for yourself and your family, and what is there to do but call in a few worthy friends to share it? Shirley MacGregor, who developed the recipe years ago when she started out in catering, packs the super-savory spread into "fat little pots or jars" she finds at yard sales. Once I filled up some beloved French onion soup crocks but resisted giving them away. Then I thought about the giving-and-receiving thing, and which one is more blessed, so I gave one to my mother, who naturally gave the empty crock back.*

2 pounds chicken livers	3 bay leaves
5 tablespoons chopped fresh parsley	2 onions, cut into chunks
1 tablespoon dried thyme	1 cup (2 sticks) butter, melted
1 garlic clove, chopped	Juice of ½ lemon
	1 teaspoon salt

Put the chicken livers, 3 tablespoons of the parsley, thyme, garlic, bay leaves, and water to cover in a large skillet over medium-high heat and bring to a boil. Reduce the heat to medium-low and simmer for 20 minutes. Drain, reserving about 1 cup of the liquid. Puree the solids in a food processor with the onions, melted butter, lemon juice, remaining 2 tablespoons parsley, and salt, until smooth as a smelt, as Shirley puts it. If the mixture seems heavy, add some of the reserved liquid, bit by bit. Fill jars, pots, or crocks with the pâté. Cover and keep chilled for up to 1 week. Serve with toast points. According to Shirley, any other kind of cracker would detract from its elegance. But I'm telling you, is it ever good on Wheat Thins.

Delicious Wishes

Russian Mushroom Caviar

Makes about 1 cup

If you can get your hands on *a loaf of rustic Russian rye or some thin pumpernickel, serve it with this spread, which Diane Williams tells us is "quite authentic in the Russian community" around Cornell University, where she works in the Russian literature department. It's a cinch to make for festive occasions.*

2 tablespoons olive oil
1 medium onion, minced
2 garlic cloves, minced
½ pound white mushrooms, chopped
1 tablespoon fresh lemon juice

1 tablespoon snipped fresh chives
1 tablespoon sour cream
Salt and freshly ground black pepper

Heat the oil in a large skillet over medium heat and sauté the onion and garlic until limp and translucent, about 5 minutes. Add the mushrooms and cook until they soften and release their juices, about 5 minutes. Stir in the lemon juice, chives, sour cream, and salt and pepper to taste. Transfer the "caviar" to a small serving bowl, cover, and chill. Serve with melba toast, crackers, or thin slices of pumpernickel or Russian rye.

Tuscany Toast

Makes 12 toasts

Sue Crouse calls this *her "recipe find of the year." These toasts can launch a party, accompany a rustic soup supper, or stand alone as a quick lunch. I give you a recipe for your own pesto so you can play the gourmet, but the supermarket's fancy food section is usually most obliging.*

Pesto

- 2 cups fresh basil leaves
- ³/₄ cup freshly grated Parmesan cheese
- ¹/₄ cup pine nuts or chopped walnuts
- 4 garlic cloves
- ¹/₂ cup olive oil

- 12 ¹/₄-inch-thick slices French or Italian bread
- ¹/₄ cup sun-dried tomato bits
- ¹/₂ cup freshly grated Parmesan cheese

To make the pesto: Put the basil, cheese, pine nuts or walnuts, and garlic in a blender jar. Slowly drizzling in the oil, whir until the pesto is smooth and thick but not runny.

Preheat the oven to 400°F.

Put the bread on a cookie sheet and spread one side of each slice with about 1 tablespoon of the pesto. Sprinkle the sun-dried tomato bits over the pesto and top with the cheese. Bake for 8 minutes, or until crisp and golden. Serve hot.

 **Note**

The pesto, with a thin layer of olive oil on top, keeps well for 2 weeks in a covered jar in the fridge.

Party Cheese Crackers

Makes 6½ dozen crackers

A snazzy alternative *to store-bought crackers, these rich little devils sport a whiff of chili powder, the haunting flavor of blue cheese, and that friendly, colorful nut, the pistachio.*

1½ cups grated cheddar cheese (about 6 ounces), at room temperature

1 cup (2 sticks) butter, softened

½ cup crumbled blue cheese (about 2 ounces), at room temperature

1 teaspoon chili powder

½ cup chopped salted pistachios

2 cups all-purpose flour

Using a wooden spoon, cream the cheddar, butter, blue cheese, and chili powder in a medium bowl. Stir in the pistachios. Sift the flour into the cheese mixture and work it in until well blended.

Form the dough into three 9-inch-long logs. Wrap the logs in wax paper or plastic wrap and chill for 2 hours, or until firm.

Preheat the oven to 350°F.

Slice the logs into ⅜-inch-thick rounds. Put the rounds 1 inch apart on ungreased cookie

 **Note**

For a savory surprise, sneak a few cheese crackers into the holiday assortment of homemade cookies you share with neighbors and friends. They're a simple cure for the monotony of the abundant sweets of the season.

sheets. Bake for 10 to 14 minutes, or until barely browned on the edges. Serve warm or at room temperature. Store the crackers in an airtight tin for up to 2 weeks.

"My friends Carol and Kim and I have baked thousands of pounds of Christmas cookies and sold them in Cookie Walks to benefit our school. We don't do the benefit anymore, but we still bake our brains out together."

— Evelyn Seymour

Randy's
Mushroom Tart

Serves 8 as a first course; more as a nibble

The spooky spore, *that mystical, mycological, fleshy, funky fungus, comes out of the damp darkness into* Cook & Tell's *broad daylight, only to go undercover again inside a piecrust. Randy Decoteau spins off an herbed mushroom variation of Don Cavanaugh's Cream Cheese and Hot Pepper Jelly Tart (page 234) to ensure variety on your platter of party hors d'oeuvres.*

1 tablespoon olive oil	½ teaspoon dry mustard
1 tablespoon butter	½ teaspoon dried thyme
1 medium onion, chopped	Dash of Worcestershire sauce
½ celery rib with leaves, minced	Dash of sweet rice vinegar
12 medium white mushrooms, sliced	Salt and freshly ground black pepper
2 tablespoons chopped fresh parsley	Pastry for a single-crust 9- or 10-inch pie (see Fail-Safe Piecrust, page 311)

Heat the oil and butter in a large skillet over medium heat and sauté the onion and celery until limp and translucent, about 5 minutes. Add the mushrooms, parsley, mustard, thyme, Worcestershire, vinegar, and salt and pepper to taste and sauté for 3 minutes, or until the mushrooms give up their juices.

Preheat the oven to 400°F.

Roll out the pastry into a 10-to-12-inch circle and transfer it to an ungreased cookie sheet. Using a slotted spoon and leaving behind as much liquid as possible, spread the mushroom mixture over half of the pastry. Moisten the edge of the pastry with water and fold it over the filling. Crimp the edge with a fork and cut vents. Bake for 20 minutes, or until the pastry is lightly browned. Serve hot, warm, or at room temperature, in wedges as a first course or in smaller pieces as hors d'oeuvres.

Cream Cheese and Hot Pepper Jelly Tart

Serves 6 as a first course; more as a nibble

Don Cavanaugh makes this appetizer *with a prefab crust. I will not back down on my claim that nothing beats a good homemade piecrust, but I give you Don's recipe the way he gave it to all of us, with a bow to Pillsbury. (I also give you Fail-Safe Piecrust on page 311). The cream cheese is a mellow modifier for the peppy, peppery jelly. The whole construction broadly hints that the dinner to follow is going to be good!*

1 store-bought refrigerated piecrust

4 ounces cream cheese, at room temperature
About ⅓ cup hot pepper jelly

Preheat the oven to 375°F.
Put the piecrust on an ungreased cookie sheet. Spread the cream cheese over half of the crust, leaving a ½-inch margin at the edge. Top with the jelly. Moisten the edge with water, fold the crust over the filling, and crimp the edges with a fork. Cut slits for vents. Bake for 20 to 25 minutes, or until golden. Cool briefly and serve in wedges as a first course or in smaller pieces as hors d'oeuvres.

Turkish Boereks

Makes 10 to 12 turnovers

A Turkish cookbook *Alice Peters brought me from her travels provided the inspiration for my Americanized rendition of a Middle Eastern savory turnover. Put a plateful of these plump pastries on the holiday sideboard and invite guests to discover the hidden secret within—a cheese-and-herb filling that's as easy to put together as its flaky wrap.*

Pastry

- 4 ounces cream cheese
- 8 tablespoons (1 stick) butter
- 2 tablespoons heavy cream
- 1¼ cups all-purpose flour
- ½ teaspoon salt

a Turkish boerek knows how to keep a secret

Filling

- 1 tablespoon butter
- 3 scallions (white and light green parts), chopped
- 1 cup grated cheddar cheese (about 4 ounces)
- ⅓ cup cottage cheese
- 1 large egg, lightly beaten
- ¼ cup chopped fresh parsley
- ½ teaspoon dried dill weed
- Salt and freshly ground black pepper

- 2 large egg yolks, lightly beaten

To make the pastry: Using an electric mixer, beat the cream cheese, butter, and cream in a medium bowl until smooth and creamy. Using a wooden spoon, work in the flour and salt. Shape into a thick disk, wrap in plastic wrap, and chill for about 30 minutes.

Roll out the dough ⅛ inch thick on a floured surface and cut it into 5-inch disks, using a saucer or other round thing about that size. Gather up the scraps and reroll for maximum circle output.

Preheat the oven to 350°F.

To make the filling: Melt the butter in a medium skillet over medium heat and sauté the scallions until limp, about 5 minutes. Remove from the heat and stir in the cheddar, cottage cheese, egg, parsley, dill, and salt and pepper to taste.

Put a spoonful of the filling on each dough disk, moisten the edges with water, and fold in half over the filling. Crimp the edges with a fork. Put the boereks on an ungreased cookie sheet and brush with the egg yolks. Bake for 20 to 25 minutes, or until golden. Serve warm or cold.

Note

This rich pastry will be even flakier if the filled boereks are chilled, on the cookie sheet, for 30 minutes before baking. Brush with the egg yolks just before baking.

Christmas Eve Oyster Stew

Serves 4

Every Christmas Eve, *we fix a sumptuous soup supper, starring the elegant oyster. Yes, there's cream and butter. The road to sumptuosity is paved with cream and butter. Come on! It's Christmas!*

4 tablespoons (½ stick) butter

1 cup thinly sliced celery

¼ cup finely chopped green bell pepper

3 tablespoons finely chopped onion

1 pint shucked fresh oysters, drained (reserve the liquid)

2 cups homemade chicken stock or canned chicken broth

Salt and freshly ground white pepper

2 cups light cream or milk

Melt the butter in a medium saucepan over medium heat and sauté the celery, bell pepper, and onion until the onion is limp and translucent, about 5 minutes. Add the oysters, reduce the heat to low, and sauté for 3 to 4 minutes, or until their edges curl.

Stir in the reserved oyster liquid, stock or broth, and salt and white pepper to taste and heat gently. Heat the cream or milk in a separate small saucepan, then add it to the oyster mixture.

Don't expect the stew to be thick. We're talking oysters and cream here, and we like it fashionably thin. Serve hot.

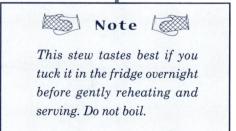

Note

This stew tastes best if you tuck it in the fridge overnight before gently reheating and serving. Do not boil.

Cold Curried Shrimp Salad with Chutney Aspic

Serves 4

My mother-in-law, *who was my gourmet guru, often included this extra-special dish on the menus of her gala suppers, where artists and writers would gather. This aspic-ringed salad always makes a grand impression and never seems dated.*

Chutney Aspic

1½ envelopes unflavored gelatin
1 cup homemade beef or chicken stock or canned beef or chicken broth (or 1 bouillon cube + 1 cup water)
2 tablespoons mango chutney (cut up any big chunks)
Dash of salt
¾ cup orange juice
1 tablespoon fresh lime juice

Cold Curried Shrimp Salad

1 cup mayonnaise
1 tablespoon curry powder
Salt
1 cup cooked shrimp, peeled, deveined, and cut into small pieces
½ cup chopped celery
¼ cup capers, drained
1 large hard-boiled egg, chopped
2 tablespoons chopped onion

To make the aspic: Soften the gelatin in ¼ cup cold water in a medium bowl. Bring the stock or broth to a boil in a small saucepan and add it to the gelatin along with the chutney and salt, stirring until dissolved. Stir in the orange juice and lime juice. Pour into a wet 1-quart ring mold and chill until firm.

To make the salad: Combine the mayonnaise, curry powder, and salt to taste in a small bowl. Combine the shrimp, celery, capers, hard-boiled egg, and onion in a medium bowl. Add the mayonnaise mixture and gently toss to coat. At serving time, unmold the aspic onto a platter and fill the center with the shrimp salad. Put the over-flow into a small bowl beside the platter. Serve cold.

Crab Imperial for Commoners

Serves 4 to 6

A recipe from *Christiana Campbell's Tavern in Williamsburg, Virginia, sent me searching for fresh backfin lump crabmeat. I had to put in a special order with my fish man, because I wanted it to be so right, so fresh, so Chesapeake. Hang the expense.*

The finished product was nothing special and too fussy anyway. I made it again, using canned supermarket crabmeat from Thailand, fiddling until I had something more suited to commoners than royalty.

1 pound crabmeat (three 6-ounce cans work fine)	1 tablespoon capers, drained
2/3 cups fine, dry bread crumbs (made from 4-day-old bread slices whirred in a blender, or store-bought)	3/4 cup mayonnaise
	1 tablespoon Worcestershire sauce
	1 tablespoon prepared mustard (any kind)
1/4 cup finely chopped green bell pepper	Dash of Tabasco sauce
1–2 tablespoons chopped pimiento	2 tablespoons (1/4 stick) butter

Preheat the oven to 350°F.
Combine the crabmeat, 1/3 cup of the bread crumbs, bell pepper, pimiento, capers, 1/2 cup of the mayonnaise, Worcestershire, mustard,

and Tabasco in a large bowl. Pile the mixture lightly into individual ramekins or, if you don't mind the mixed metaphor, in giant oven-safe scallop shells. Dab each portion with some of the remaining $1/4$ cup mayonnaise, cover with the remaining $1/3$ cup bread crumbs, and dot with the butter. Bake for 30 minutes, or until browned and sizzling. Serve hot.

Turkey Roasted with Whole Fruit and Hot Sausage Stuffing

Serves 8

We bring you now, *in the most exquisite detail, the simplest way to cook the most delicious turkey for the best Thanksgiving ever. The stuffing cooks separately, alongside. To save time on T-day, you can make the stuffing ahead and freeze it.*

1 12-pound turkey (Use a bigger bird if your group is large.)
Salt
1 orange, pricked all over with a fork
1 lemon, pricked all over with a fork
1 onion
1 celery rib, cut into several pieces

A small bunch fresh parsley, sage, rosemary, and thyme
8 tablespoons (1 stick) butter, softened
Freshly ground black pepper

Hot Sausage Stuffing (recipe follows)

Preheat the oven to 325°F.

Rinse the turkey inside and out with cold water and pat dry with paper towels. Salt the inside of the turkey and stuff it with the orange, lemon, onion, and celery. Stow the bunch of herbs in any available interior cranny. Rub the bird all over with the butter (you may

not need it all) and sprinkle it with salt and pepper to taste. Place the turkey breast on a rack in a roasting pan and pour in 1 cup water. Roast until a thermometer stuck into the thickest part of a thigh registers 180°F, about 4 hours. After 1 hour, start basting whenever you think of it. Discard the fruit and vegetable stuffing before carving and serving, and bring on the Hot Sausage Stuffing.

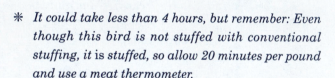

Notes

✳ *It could take less than 4 hours, but remember: Even though this bird is not stuffed with conventional stuffing, it is stuffed, so allow 20 minutes per pound and use a meat thermometer.*

✳ *We've also done this turkey-stuffed-with-fruit business the way Jacqui Sadler does it, using a "good, green apple" instead of the lemon, with all the fruit and the onion quartered. The basting liquid and the gravy derived from all the fruity ballast—press those fruit quarters into the juices while the turkey rests—are nothing short of elegant.*

✳ *Laura White squeezes the orange over the turkey before consigning it to the bird's interior. "I think it adds moistness," she says, "and I think you can taste the difference." Well, it certainly does. And you really can.*

Hot Sausage Stuffing

Serves 10 to 12

When the first thought of Thanksgiving *crosses your mind, make Betsy Allport's stuffing, pack it into a baking dish, and put it in the freezer. Thaw and bake on Thanksgiving Day. Or make it on the very day, if you like.*

1 pound hot Italian sausages, casings discarded

1 1-pound package unseasoned stuffing mix (not cubes)

3 large onions, finely chopped

8 celery ribs, finely chopped

½ cup chopped fresh parsley

8 tablespoons (1 stick) butter, melted

2 large eggs, lightly beaten

¼ cup chopped fresh sage or 2 tablespoons dried

1 tablespoon chopped fresh thyme or 2 teaspoons dried

A few shakes of poultry seasoning

Salt and freshly ground black pepper

Milk

Preheat the oven to 350°F. Heat a large skillet over medium-high heat and brown the sausage, breaking it up in small bits, until cooked through. Drain off the fat and cool the sausage slightly.

Combine the sausage, stuffing mix, onions, celery, parsley, butter, eggs, sage, thyme, poultry seasoning, and salt and pepper to taste in a large bowl. Add about ¹/₂ cup milk, a little at a time, until the stuffing's consistency is to your liking. Put the stuffing in an oven-to-table baking dish. Bake for 25 to 35 minutes, or until heated through. Or cover and store in the freezer for up to 3 months and thaw before baking.

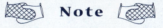

Note

To prevent the stuffing from drying out, baste with the turkey juices while baking. (If you're baking the stuffing after a sojourn in the freezer and there's no turkey in sight, use chicken broth.)

It's a Wonderful Meal

coming soon to a dining room near you!

Cranberry-Glazed Pork Roast

Serves 16

New England's beloved berries *are the basis for the sauce that enrobes this succulent roast, the perfect centerpiece for a festive winter menu. The recipe is Randy Decoteau's adaptation of one from* Eating Well, *with tinkering by* Cook & Tell. *We recommend Squab-bage (page 217) and mashed potatoes as accompaniments. Grandma Schmidt's Apple Pie (page 314) is a grand dessert choice.*

Cranberry Glaze

- 1 1-pound can whole-berry cranberry sauce
- 2 tablespoons apple juice
- 2 tablespoons fresh lemon juice
- 2 tablespoons cornstarch
- 1 teaspoon sugar
- ¼ teaspoon ground cinnamon
   Pinch of salt

- 1 4-pound boneless pork loin
   Salt and freshly ground
      black pepper

Preheat the oven to 325°F.

To make the glaze: Combine the ingredients in a small saucepan over medium heat and stir until thickened. Set aside and keep warm.

Put the pork in a shallow baking dish and sprinkle with salt and pepper to taste. Roast for 45 minutes. Spoon about ½ cup of the glaze over the roast and roast for 45 minutes more, or until the interior

temperature registers 155° to 160°F on a meat thermometer. Add more glaze from time to time, if necessary. There's plenty. Let the roast stand for 10 minutes before slicing. Serve with the remaining warm cranberry glaze.

> ### Note
>
> *The rule of thumb for roast pork is 30 minutes per pound, but you must watch. The roast could be done sooner than that, as implied by the 90-minute total mentioned in the instructions. Anything bigger than a 4-pound loin will take forever to cook.*

Fruit Juice–Basted Ham

Serves 10 to 12

Phyllis Gimbel cooks ham this way, *except for the juice part, which I grafted onto her recipe. She prefers Cook's brand hams. An unnamed store-brand specimen always works for me. The finished product is incredibly tender and gently flavored, resembling in no way the salty-smoked southern variety. Two-Tone Mashed Potatoes with Goat Cheese (page 214) and Glazed Carrots (page 213) are great go-withs.*

1 precooked ham (shank or butt)	3 cups fruit juice: apple, orange,
Whole cloves	pineapple, or a combination
Scant 2 tablespoons light	2 tablespoons all-purpose flour
brown sugar	

Put the ham and water to cover in a Dutch oven or other large, heavy-bottomed pot and bring to a boil over high heat. Reduce the heat to medium-low and simmer, covered, for 3 hours. Cool the ham in its broth and refrigerate until you're ready to bake it — several hours, overnight, or whatever.

Preheat the oven to 350°F.

Drain the ham and discard the broth. Remove and discard the rind and most of the fat from the ham. Put the ham in a deep roasting pan; you don't need a rack.

Score the ham in the customary diamond pattern and stud the intersections with cloves. Dissolve the brown sugar in ³/₄ cup boiling water in a medium bowl and add the fruit juice. Reserve ⅓ cup of the juice mixture. Pour the remaining juice mixture over the ham, to a depth of about 1 inch. Bake for 1 hour, basting every 15 minutes. Transfer the ham to a platter and cover loosely with foil to keep it warm while you make the sauce.

Transfer the juices from the roasting pan to a medium saucepan and bring to a boil over high heat. Combine the flour and the reserved ⅓ cup juice mixture in a jar, screw on the lid, and shake until smooth. Stir the flour mixture into the ham juices, reduce the heat to medium-low, and simmer until thickened. Serve immediately with the ham.

Pepper-Crusted Filet Mignon

Makes 1 serving; multiplies easily

"My all-time favorite COOK & TELL recipe, based on having made it fifty times, is Pepper-Crusted Filet Mignon. I make it with eye of the round roast for economy. I used store-bought coarse-ground pepper — it sticks like glue and toasts up nicely for an added dimension of flavor."

— Susan Delaney-Mech

Mary, the meat lady at our local market, *put me onto this snazzy treatment for those satiny hunks of beef that are way too classy to be called mere steaks. I recommend this dish to all who aspire to grillmeister status. Requiring no skills beyond the ability to cut a radius from the center to the edge of a filet, Mary's beef treatment is an elegant, no-hassle way to impress your friends. And for a grand indoor-outdoor Christmas dinner, put on your woolly Santa suit and grill the filets outdoors while a potato casserole, and everything else on your Christmas menu, cooks inside.*

1 6-to-8-ounce filet mignon
   per person
1 garlic clove per filet, halved
1 tablespoon whole black
   peppercorns per filet

   Olive oil or vegetable oil
1 small wedge Camembert or
   Brie cheese per filet

Preheat a gas grill on high for 10 minutes.
Using a sharp knife, make 2 slits in the sides of each filet and stick a garlic half into each slit. Coarsely crush the peppercorns between 2 sheets of wax paper, using a mallet or the bottom of a heavy skillet to crush but not grind them. Spread the crushed pepper evenly over the wax paper. Brush each filet all over with oil and coat it on all sides with the crushed pepper.

Reduce the grill heat to medium-high and cook the filets for 6 minutes per side for gorgeously rare, or until done to your liking. Place the filets on heated plates and, with a sharp knife, make a radial cut from the center of each filet to the edge. Spread it open gently and insert a wedge of cheese into the opening. Voilà! The cheese melts into place. Serve immediately.

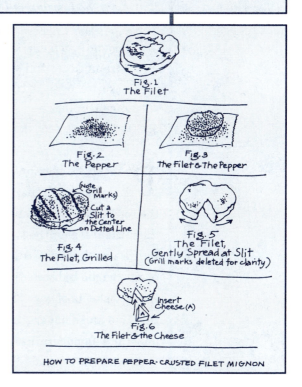

Note

The recipe specifies a gas grill. Of course, you can do this on a charcoal grill. As for timing, make a sneaky poke into the meat with your sharp knife to see how you're doing. You're on your own. Go for it!

Fig. 1
The Filet

Fig. 2
The Pepper

Fig. 3
The Filet & The Pepper

(Note Grill Marks)
Cut a Slit to the Center on Dotted Line
Fig. 4
The Filet, Grilled

Fig. 5
The Filet, Gently Spread at Slit
(Grill marks deleted for clarity)

Insert Cheese (A)
Fig. 6
The Filet & the Cheese

HOW TO PREPARE PEPPER-CRUSTED FILET MIGNON

Roast Tenderloin of Beef
with Horseradish Cream

Serves 12

If you're like me, *you need a pretty good excuse to spend nine bucks a pound for a hunk of meat. Here it is: Phyllis Gimbel's scrumptious and cinchy roast beef. Invite your best beau or lady and another couple for a double date, or hog the whole thing for just the two of you. Fluffy baked potatoes and Asparagus ASAP (page 204) are suitably stylish, no-fuss accompaniments.*

1 3-pound beef tenderloin, trimmed of all fat and silver-skin (see Note), at room temperature

3–4 garlic cloves, halved vertically

2 tablespoons (¼ stick) butter, softened

Freshly ground black pepper

Horseradish Cream (recipe follows)

Preheat the oven to 500°F.

Using a small, sharp knife, make little slits here and there along the top of the tenderloin and stuff each slit with a garlic half. Spread the butter all over the tenderloin and sprinkle it with pepper to taste. Put the tenderloin in a roasting pan—but not on a rack. Put the pan in the oven and immediately reduce the oven temperature to 450°F. Roast for 45 minutes. That's it. No matter the size of the tenderloin, the time and temperature are the same. Remove from the oven and let stand for 15 minutes before slicing. Serve with Horseradish Cream.

Horseradish Cream

Makes about 2½ cups

1 cup heavy cream
½ cup prepared horseradish

Whip the cream in a medium bowl until soft peaks form. Fold in the horseradish and serve with the tenderloin.

Note

Have the butcher remove the silverskin. Or make very shallow cuts across the silverskin every inch or so along the edge of the tenderloin, as you would score the fat on the edge of a steak to keep it from curling. I have the butcher tie the tenderloin for fairly round slices.

Simple Shepherd's Pie
for Christmas Eve

Serves 6

The homey goodness of the dish *Jean Black makes for an appreciative family every Christmas Eve is its most endearing quality. Those shepherds of yore had a lot of listening to do on that night of nights. They didn't bother to fix a gourmet meal, and neither should you. I fiddled a bit with the recipe, adding ketchup and bouillon (and the paprika is an extravagance that looks especially good here), but I tried to keep it simple.*

3 tablespoons butter, plus more for the casserole dish	1 pound ground beef
3 large potatoes, peeled	¼ cup dehydrated minced onion
½–1 cup milk	1 tablespoon all-purpose flour
Salt and freshly ground black pepper	1 beef bouillon cube
2 tablespoons vegetable oil	3 tablespoons ketchup
	1 1-pound can cream-style corn
	Paprika

Preheat the oven to 350°F. Butter a 1½-quart casserole dish. Boil the potatoes in a medium saucepan of water until cooked through, about 35 minutes. Drain. Mash the potatoes by hand with the milk and 3 tablespoons butter in a medium bowl. Season with salt and pepper to taste and set aside.

Heat the oil in a large skillet over medium-high heat and brown the ground beef until cooked through, about 5 minutes. Stir in the dehydrated onion, flour, bouillon cube, and ketchup and cook for 2 minutes more. Add 1 cup water, reduce the heat to medium-low, and simmer for 15 minutes, or until thickened. Season with salt and pepper to taste.

Put the ground-beef mixture in the prepared dish and pour the corn over it. Pile on the mashed potatoes and sprinkle them with paprika to taste. Bake for 35 minutes, or until the potatoes are lightly browned.

Note

You can cover and chill the assembled casserole for later baking. Bring it to room temperature before baking at 350°F until heated through.

Tourtière
(French-Canadian Meat Pie)

Serves 6

Rich and satisfying enough *for a country-style Christmas dinner, tourtière is a French-Canadian meat pie that's apt to be on the Québecois menu almost anytime during the holiday season. Randy Decoteau traces the recipe's lineage from his great-grandmother, Cecilia, to his grandmother, Rose, to his mother, Jean.* Then Cook & Tell *got into the act, insisted on mostly pork, and introduced a hint of Tabasco sauce, which is probably not authentic, but at least it's Cajun. And I'm French on my mother's side, so I'm entitled.*

1 pound ground pork	¹/₄ teaspoon freshly ground
¹/₂ pound ground veal or lean	black pepper
ground beef	Salt
1 medium onion, minced	Tabasco sauce (optional)
¹/₄ cup minced celery	¹/₂ cup soft, fresh bread crumbs
1 garlic clove, minced	Pastry for a double-crust
¹/₂ teaspoon poultry seasoning	9-inch pie (see Fail-Safe
¹/₂ teaspoon ground cinnamon	Piecrust, page 311)
¹/₂ teaspoon ground nutmeg	Cream or milk, for brushing
¹/₄ teaspoon ground cloves	the crust

Put the pork, veal or beef, onion, celery, garlic, poultry seasoning, cinnamon, nutmeg, cloves, pepper, salt to taste, and ³/₄ cup boiling water in a large skillet over medium heat. Simmer, partially covered and stirring frequently, for 30 minutes, or until the pork has lost its pinkness and the juices are thickened. Remove from the heat. Drain and reserve the juices; discard any fat. Season to taste with the Tabasco, if using. Stir in the bread crumbs and reserved juices.

Preheat the oven to 350°F.

Roll out half of the pastry and line a pie plate. Trim, leaving a ¹/₂-inch overhang. Fill the pastry with the meat mixture. Roll out the top crust, cut vents, and fit it on the pie. Crimp and seal the edges. Brush the top with cream or milk. Bake for 45 minutes, or until the top crust is golden brown. Serve hot.

Raspberry Green Beans

Serves 4

The dab of raspberry jam is *Betty McCreary's inspiration. I did her one better with a raspberry salsa I concocted, after a jar of raspberry salsa I bought disappeared almost as soon as I opened it.*

1 pound green beans, trimmed
  Salt
2 teaspoons butter
2 teaspoons olive oil

1 tablespoon raspberry jam or Raspberry Salsa (recipe follows)

Cook the beans in a medium saucepan of boiling salted water until barely tender, 7 to 9 minutes. Drain, plunge them into cold water to stop the cooking, and drain again. Chill the beans until it's time to eat.

   Heat the butter and oil in a large skillet over medium heat. Add the beans and reheat, shaking the skillet and stirring. Let the beans brown slightly. Serve the glistening beans with the raspberry jam or Raspberry Salsa on top. As it melts, gently stir it in.

Raspberry Salsa

Makes about 2 cups

1 cup fresh raspberries
1 cup canned stewed tomatoes, with their juice
1/3 cup finely chopped onion
1 mild green chile (fresh or canned), chopped

1/4 cup packed light brown sugar
1 garlic clove, minced
1 teaspoon ground cumin
1/2 teaspoon salt
  Vinegar or fresh lemon juice

Using a fork, mash the raspberries in a medium bowl and stir in the tomatoes, onion, chile, brown sugar, garlic, cumin, and salt. No cooking! Add vinegar or lemon juice little by little, to taste. Serve cold.

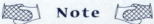 **Note**

Raspberry Salsa is also yummy served with grilled fish, hamburgers, hash, and boiled shrimp. If all else fails, scoop it up with corn chips or raw vegetables. It keeps refrigerated for 1 week.

Roast Chrysanthemum Onions

Serves 4 or 5

Don't put that jar of raspberry jam *away just yet. Consider this slightly upscale way with onions, passed to us by Marion Escoffier, from her son, Marcel. When the season is right, Vidalias are wonderful done up this way. Marion loves apple butter in place of raspberry jam!*

3 tablespoons butter	5 tablespoons raspberry jam
10 small onions	or jelly
¼ cup homemade chicken or beef stock or canned chicken or beef broth	

Preheat the oven to 450°F. Use a little of the butter to grease a medium baking dish.

Peel the onions and trim off the root ends so they will stand up. Make 2 crisscross cuts in each onion, ending about ³⁄₄ inch from the bottom. Put the onions in the prepared dish, root end down. Sprinkle the stock or broth over the onions, dot each one with butter, and top each one with ½ tablespoon raspberry jam. Cover with foil, crimping carefully for an airtight seal. Roast for 1 hour, or until tender when pierced with a fork. Serve hot.

Roasted Tarragon Potatoes and Carrots

Serves 6

If you've got a couple of potatoes *and an oven that goes up to 450°F, you're almost home with this easy recipe. And if you're inspired to wrap up all this stuff in foil packets and cook it on the grill, give yourself a pat on the back.*

4 large potatoes, each cut into 8 wedges	½ teaspoon dried tarragon
4 medium carrots, peeled and cut into 1½-inch lengths	½ teaspoon freshly ground black pepper
2 tablespoons olive oil	Coarse salt (plain salt will do)

Preheat the oven to 450°F.
Toss the potatoes and carrots in a large bowl with the oil, tarragon, and pepper. Spread the vegetables on a nonstick jelly-roll pan and roast until tender and well browned, about 30 minutes, turning the vegetables or shaking the pan occasionally. Sprinkle with salt to taste. Serve hot.

"Kudos for the fabulous Roasted Tarragon Potatoes and Carrots. I love the tarragon with the roasted roots! It was something I would never have thought of, and it worked perfectly."

— Don Cavanaugh

Tip

On baking potatoes: Paul Dupuis strings fork-pricked potatoes on a barbecue skewer when baking them for a large group—about 6 to a skewer—"so much easier to put them in or take them out of the oven," says Practical Paul.

Barley Pilaf

Serves 4

Here's one of Don Cavanaugh's favorite *and most versatile sit-down side dishes. He won't mind it a bit if you substitute cinnamon and curry powder for the cumin and coriander and send in dried cherries or cranberries for the raisins.*

2 tablespoons butter	½ teaspoon ground coriander
1 medium onion, chopped	3¾ cups homemade beef stock,
⅔ cup cashews	canned beef broth, or
½ cup raisins	water (or 3 beef bouillon
½ cup chopped dried apricots	cubes + 3¾ cups water)
¾ cup uncooked pearl barley	Salt and freshly ground
½ teaspoon ground cumin	black pepper

Melt the butter in a medium saucepan over medium heat and sauté the onion until limp and translucent, about 5 minutes. Add the cashews, raisins, and apricots and sauté until coated with butter and the fruits are slightly softened, about 3 minutes. Add the barley and sauté until it starts to turn golden and begins to smell nice, about 3 minutes. Stir in the cumin and coriander and cook for 30 seconds.

Meanwhile, bring the stock, broth, or water to a boil in a separate medium saucepan over high heat. Add it to the barley mixture. Reduce the heat to medium-low, cover, and cook, stirring occasionally, for about 40 minutes, or until the liquid is absorbed and the barley is tender. Remove from the heat, uncover, and drape a dishtowel over the pan to prevent the steam from condensing and dropping back onto the pilaf. Put the cover back on and let the pilaf stand for 5 to 10 minutes, or until dried out a bit. Season with salt and pepper to taste. Serve hot.

Baked French Toast

Serves 6

The eggs, milk, and bread *spend the night tucked into the fridge while we sleep. In the morning, the mixture goes into the oven, to emerge, browned and sweet, as French toast.*

Thank Maria Doelp, who plays occasional innkeeper at a friend's bed-and-breakfast, for this cheery, good-morning dish she sometimes serves to guests. I get credit for the Christmasy cranberries.

8 tablespoons (1 stick) butter	1½ cups milk
1 cup packed light brown sugar	5 large eggs
2 tablespoons light corn syrup	1 teaspoon vanilla extract
6–9 1-inch-thick slices French or Italian bread	⅓ cup dried cranberries

Melt the butter in a flameproof 9-by-13-inch baking pan over medium-low heat. Add the brown sugar and corn syrup and stir until dissolved. Put in as many bread slices as you can fit tightly into the pan. Flip to coat both sides with the butter mixture.

Beat the milk, eggs, and vanilla in a medium bowl. Pour over the bread, sprinkle with the cranberries, and cover the pan with plastic wrap. Refrigerate overnight.

Baked French Toast

In the morning, preheat the oven to 350°F.

Remove the plastic wrap from the pan and bake for 30 minutes, or until puffed and golden. Cut into serving pieces with the side of a spatula and serve hot.

One way to lay out Italian Bread Slices in 9"x13" pan →

Orange-Butterscotch Coffee Cake

Serves 9

During the holiday season, *chances are there'll be folks using the guest room. When they come down for breakfast, you'll want to serve them something special, something that says, "Welcome!" Linda Brewer, one of our island's good cooks, recommends this recipe from her mother. Oats, orange zest, and brown sugar give this coffee cake the flavor of comfort and friendship.*

8 tablespoons (1 stick) butter or margarine, softened, plus more for the pan
1½ cups all-purpose flour, plus more for the pan
1 cup granulated sugar
1 large egg
1 teaspoon vanilla extract
1½ teaspoons baking powder
½ teaspoon ground cinnamon

½ teaspoon salt
1 cup milk
¾ cup old-fashioned or quick-cooking rolled oats

Topping

¼ cup packed light brown sugar
1 tablespoon all-purpose flour
2 teaspoons grated fresh orange zest
1 tablespoon butter, melted

Preheat the oven to 350°F. Butter and flour an 8-inch square baking pan.
Cream the 8 tablespoons butter and sugar in a large bowl until

fluffy. Stir in the egg and vanilla. Sift the 1½ cups flour, baking powder, cinnamon, and salt into a medium bowl and add to the butter mixture alternately with the milk. Stir in the oats just until combined. Pour the batter into the prepared pan.

To make the topping: Combine the ingredients in a small bowl and sprinkle over the batter.

Bake for 40 to 45 minutes, or until the cake springs back when gently pressed in the center. Cool in the pan for 15 minutes before serving.

Linzertorte

Serves 10

Chef Fritz Blank, *of the Philadelphia restaurant Deux Chemi-nées, is back with Linzertorte. Rich with butter and ground almonds, glistening with raspberry jam, and mightily spiced with cinnamon, Fritz's version is a spectacular centerpiece for the holiday dessert table. "The 'shortness' of the crust," says the chef, "is the secret that makes this recipe the best I have ever sampled." The processor makes short work of the dough, and the fridge is your friend here, keeping the dough workable. I'm not kidding about all that cinnamon; 2 tablespoons is the correct amount.*

9 tablespoons unsalted butter, softened, plus more for the pan

⅔ cup sugar

1 cup blanched or unblanched almonds, ground

1 cup all-purpose flour

2 tablespoons ground cinnamon

1 large egg

6 heaping tablespoons seedless raspberry jam (see Note)

Confectioners' sugar

Whir the unsalted butter and sugar in a food processor until light and fluffy. Add the ground almonds, flour, cinnamon, and egg and whir until the mixture clumps together; do not overwork. Working quickly, pat out the pastry into a flat disk between two sheets of wax paper and refrigerate for at least 2 hours. It's very soft, so when it's cold, it should be handled quickly. Return the pastry to the fridge between steps and whenever it becomes too sticky.

Butter a 9-inch tart pan with a removable bottom or an 8½-inch springform pan. With the pastry still between the sheets of wax paper, roll it into a circle to fit the pan, about ¼ inch thick. Peel off the top sheet and flip the pastry into the prepared tart pan, gently pressing it in place. Trim off the excess; reserve the trimmings. If using a springform pan, press the pastry up the sides about 1 inch and trim the edge; reserve the trimmings. Chill the pastry in the pan along with the trimmings for 30 minutes, or until firm.

Preheat the oven to 350°F. Spread the jam over the tart. Roll out the trimmings and cut them into ½-inch-wide strips. Crisscross the strips over the jam in a lattice pattern, gently pinching the ends of the strips into the edge of the crust. Bake for 25 minutes, or until the pastry is barely beginning to turn golden. Cool completely. Dust with confectioners' sugar. Serve in thin wedges.

 **Note**

I prefer to use raspberry jam with seeds.

Classic Plum Pudding
with Whipped Hard Sauce

Serves 8 to 12

Betty Govan has been making this great *Christmas pudding since 1941, when raisins were 29 cents a pound and dates 19 cents, as she noted when she sent the recipe to me. She found the recipe in a dairy's leaflet. It's a love of a pudding, evoking scenes of snow swirling down narrow London streets and Bob Cratchit serving the Christmas goose. The hard sauce, softened with cream and egg white, is pure inspiration.*

1½ cups fine, dry bread crumbs
1 cup milk, heated
4 large eggs, separated
¼ cup sugar
½ pound beef suet, ground
¾ cup sifted all-purpose flour
1½ teaspoons salt
½ teaspoon ground nutmeg
½ teaspoon ground cinnamon
½ pound raisins
½ pound dried currants

½ cup chopped dates
½ cup chopped candied citron or orange peel, or a combination of both (or neither, and use more of the other fruits)
¼ cup chopped dried figs
½ cup apple cider, heated

Whipped Hard Sauce (recipe follows)

Grease a pudding mold with a cover or two 13- or 15-ounce coffee cans.

Combine the bread crumbs and milk in a small bowl and let stand for 10 minutes. Beat the egg yolks with the sugar in a large bowl until thick and light-colored. Add the suet and mix well. Combine the flour, salt, nutmeg, and cinnamon in a separate large bowl. Add the raisins, currants, dates, candied citron or orange peel, and figs and stir to distribute evenly. Stir the dried-fruit mixture into the egg-yolk mixture. Add the bread-crumb mixture and the cider and mix well. Beat the egg whites in a medium bowl until stiff but not dry and fold them into the batter.

Transfer the batter to the prepared mold, then cover the mold. If using coffee cans, fill them only about three-quarters full. Fold two large sheets of wax paper twice so you have four layers that will fit over the top of each can with a 2-inch overhang. Tightly tie the wax paper onto the coffee cans with string. Place the mold or cans on a rack in a pot deep enough to accommodate them when the pot is covered. Pour in 1 inch of boiling water, cover the pot, and steam the puddings for 3 hours over heat that will maintain the water at a gentle boil. Add boiling water from time to time when the water level goes down. Serve hot with Whipped Hard Sauce.

Whipped Hard Sauce

Makes about 2 cups

4   tablespoons (½ stick) butter,
    softened
1   cup confectioners' sugar

1   large egg white
1   cup heavy cream
1   teaspoon vanilla extract

Cream the butter and sugar in a large bowl. Beat in the egg white.

Whip the cream in a medium bowl and beat into the butter mixture. Fold in the vanilla. Chill or serve immediately.

Trifle

Serves 8

The English trifle began *as a humble culinary expedient, a way to use up leftover cake, the last of the custard, and dabs of jam. Nowadays, at least in this upstart country, trifle is a big deal. You make the cake, you make the custard, you make a production out of it. With Barbara Widmayer's foolproof recipe in your portfolio, you'll earn a guaranteed reputation as a cook to be reckoned with.*

1 recipe Hot-Water Sponge
   Cake (page 324)

Custard Sauce

1½ tablespoons cornstarch
2 cups half-and-half
4 large egg yolks
½ cup sugar
1 teaspoon vanilla extract

1 cup apricot jam
⅔ cup falernum syrup or sherry
   (see Note)
1½ cups fresh strawberries,
   rinsed, hulled, and chopped,
   or one 29-ounce can pear
   halves, drained and chopped
½ cup crushed amaretti cookies
1 cup heavy cream, whipped

*"Although it's time-consuming to make the various components, this recipe goes together quickly, once you get to the assembling stage. Also, you simply **cannot** fail, and it's absolutely a hit with everyone. What more could you ask for from a dessert?"*

— Barbara Widmayer

Preheat the oven to 325°F. Line a 15-by-10-inch jelly-roll pan with wax paper, allowing the two ends of the paper to drape a bit over the ends of the pan.

To make the cake: Follow the directions for Hot-Water Sponge Cake on page 324. Spread the cake batter with a rubber spatula into the lined jelly-roll pan. Bake for about 35 minutes, or until light brown. Lift the hot cake out of the pan by the edges of the paper and cool on a rack. Set aside until ready to assemble the trifle.

To make the custard sauce: Dissolve the cornstarch in $^1/_4$ cup of the half-and-half in a small bowl. Beat the egg yolks well in a separate small bowl, then add the cornstarch mixture. Heat the remaining $1^3/_4$ cups half-and-half in a small saucepan until very hot (not boiling), then add the sugar. Remove from the heat and quickly stir 3 tablespoons of the hot cream into the yolks. Then add the remaining cream and return to the heat. Cook, stirring constantly, over medium heat for 5 minutes, or until thickened. Add the vanilla and cool.

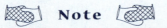

Note

Falernum syrup, which has a tropical citruslike flavor, is my teetotaling alternative to the traditional sherry. It can be found in many fancy food stores.

To assemble: Flip the cooled sponge cake onto a cutting board and peel off the paper. Cut the cake in half and place one piece on the bottom of a 2-quart Pyrex baking dish or flat-bottomed glass bowl or trifle dish. Coat with half of the jam. Combine the falernum syrup or sherry with $^1/_3$ cup water in a small bowl and sprinkle half of it over the jam. Cover with half of the strawberries or pears, then half of the amaretti crumbs. Spread half of the custard sauce over all. Repeat the layers, improvising sizes and quantities according to the shape of your container. Spread the whipped cream over the top. Cover with plastic wrap and refrigerate for several hours before serving.

Turkish Apricot Dessert
with Pistachios
and Whipped Cream

Serves 6 to 8

It's a party, and the desserts *are making their way to the buffet table. Something different, something exotic, catches a guest's eye, and you can hear the gasp of delight. The savvy host or hostess never reveals how little effort goes into such a smashing finale. The original recipe is on a yellowed scrap of a page from an old issue of* House & Garden. *I've added a garnish of pistachios, the quintessential Middle Eastern nut. Unsweetened whipped cream is the perfect pacifier, softening the richness of the flavors.*

1 pound whole dried apricots	1 cup heavy cream, softly whipped
³/₄ cup sugar	
2 tablespoons fresh lemon juice	2 tablespoons finely chopped pistachios, for garnish
³/₄ cup toasted sliced almonds, finely chopped	

Soak the apricots overnight in a medium bowl of cold water to cover by 1 inch. The next day, drain, measure the water, and add to it enough water to equal 1¹/₂ cups. Bring the water and sugar to a boil in a medium, nonreactive saucepan over medium-high heat. Add the drained apricots, reduce the heat to low, and simmer until the apricots are tender and the syrup is reduced to about $1/2$ cup, 45 to 60 minutes. Stir in the lemon juice and cook for 3 minutes more. Remove from the heat and cool. Transfer the apricot mixture to a medium serving bowl, cover the surface with the chopped almonds, and spread the whipped cream over the top. Garnish with the chopped pistachios and serve.

Note

Even salted pistachios work well here. They provide an interesting contrast to the tangy sweetness of the apricots.

Mary's Scottish Shortbread

Makes about 5 dozen cookies

Mary Ekberg's favorite cookies *bring tidings of comfort and joy to all who partake of the Christmas cookie tray's offerings. Never one to leave well enough alone, I divide up the dough and work in a few surprises.*

2 cups (4 sticks) butter, softened	2 large egg yolks
1 cup packed light brown sugar	1 teaspoon vanilla extract
½ cup granulated sugar	4 cups all-purpose flour

Cream the butter, brown sugar, and granulated sugar in a large bowl. Using a wooden spoon, work in the egg yolks and vanilla, then the flour. Chill for 1 hour.

Preheat the oven to 400°F.

Roll out a portion of the dough ⅓ inch thick on a lightly floured surface, leaving the remaining dough in the fridge. Cut into squares or other shapes and place on an ungreased cookie sheet. Continue with the remaining dough, a portion at a time. Keep re-rolling of the dough to a

---

 **Note**

For variations, divide the dough into three parts. To one part, add 1 cup finely ground salted cashews. To the second, add ½ cup finely chopped crystallized ginger. Leave the third part plain. Bake as directed.

minimum by piecing together the scraps and flattening them with the rolling pin. Bake for 10 minutes, or until just beginning to color. Cool on a rack. Store in an airtight tin for 2 to 3 weeks, or freeze for 3 months.

Brown Sugar Cut-Out Cookies

Makes 4 to 6 dozen cookies, depending on
the size of your cookie cutters

"These are the very best 'Christmas-tree cookies' you ever tasted."

— Dottie Williamson

Who doesn't love cookies *shaped like Christmas stars and angels, trees and camels, all sparkly with colored sugar? Dottie Williamson sends us her mother's recipe, beloved by family and friends. They're brown-sugar-good and oh-so-thin—the very spirit of crispness.*

2	cups packed light brown sugar	2	teaspoons baking powder
1	cup vegetable shortening	1	teaspoon baking soda
2	large eggs	½	teaspoon salt
1	teaspoon vanilla extract		Colored sugars, for decorating
4	cups all-purpose flour		

Cream the brown sugar and shortening in a large bowl. Add the eggs, 3 tablespoons cold water, and vanilla. Sift the flour, baking powder, baking soda, and salt into a medium bowl and add to the brown-sugar mixture, working it in with your hands or a wooden spoon. Wrap the dough in plastic wrap and chill for at least 2 hours or overnight.

Preheat the oven to 350°F. Line cookie sheets with foil.

Roll out a portion of the dough very thinly on a floured surface, leaving the remaining dough in the fridge. Cut out shapes with cookie cutters and sprinkle with colored sugars. Re-roll the scraps and re-cut. Using a floured spatula, transfer the cookies to the prepared cookie sheets. Bake for 6 minutes, or until the edges are barely beginning to color. Cool on a wire rack. Continue with the remaining dough. Store in an airtight tin for up to 2 weeks, or freeze for up to 3 months.

"The Brown Sugar Cut-Out Cookies were wonderful. I don't think I'll ever use my old recipe again."

—Sara Tatham

Cardamom
Refrigerator Cookies

Makes 8 to 10 dozen cookies

Cardamom, **with an aroma** *that seems almost too big for its tiny seeds and dainty pods, is the flavor signature of the festive breads, pastries, and cookies of Scandinavia. There's a haunting, sweet pungency that gently flavors cardamom-spiced cakes and cookies and makes them memorable.*

3½ cups sifted all-purpose flour
1 teaspoon baking soda
½ teaspoon salt
1 cup (2 sticks) butter or margarine, softened
1½ cups packed light brown sugar

½ cup granulated sugar
2 large eggs
1 teaspoon vanilla extract
2 teaspoons ground cardamom
1 cup finely chopped pecans

Preheat the oven to 375°F.
Sift the flour, baking soda, and salt into a medium bowl. Cream the butter, brown sugar, and granulated sugar in a large bowl. Stir in the eggs, vanilla, and cardamom. Gradually stir in half the flour mixture, then stir in the rest of the flour to form a stiff dough. Add the pecans and mix thoroughly. Transfer the dough to a floured board, divide it into thirds, and form each third into an 8-to-10-inch log. Wrap the logs in plastic wrap or wax paper and refrigerate until firm, or freeze for up to 3 months to bake another day. Cut the logs crosswise

into ¼-inch-thick slices. Bake on ungreased cookie sheets for 10 minutes, or until golden brown. Cool on a rack. Store in an airtight tin for about 1 week, or freeze for up to 2 months.

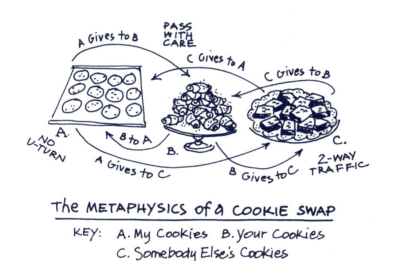

The METAPHYSICS of a COOKIE SWAP

KEY: A. My Cookies   B. Your Cookies
C. Somebody Else's Cookies

# Florentines

Makes about 2 dozen cookies

The holiday cookie array *wouldn't be complete without this lacy, elegant classic. Beyond the traditional orange peel, I've offered other fruity choices, all of which are nicely complemented by the chocolate dip at the end.*

5 tablespoons butter, plus more for the cookie sheet
½ cup heavy cream
½ cup sugar
1¼ cups finely chopped blanched almonds

¾ cup finely chopped candied orange peel, crystallized ginger, or glazed dried apricots
⅓ cup all-purpose flour
4 ounces (⅔ cup) semisweet chocolate chips

Preheat the oven to 350°F. Butter a cookie sheet. Combine 3 tablespoons of the butter, the cream, and sugar in a medium saucepan and bring to a boil. Remove from the heat and stir in the almonds; orange peel, ginger, or apricots; and flour.

Drop spoonfuls of the batterlike dough 3 inches apart on the prepared cookie sheet; they'll spread into lacy circles as they bake. Bake for 10 minutes, or until golden and set. Let cool on the cookie sheet for 5 minutes before transferring to a rack to finish cooling.

Melt the chocolate chips and the remaining 2 tablespoons butter in a bowl set over a saucepan of barely simmering (not boiling) water.

Spread the melted chocolate on the tops of the cookies, or dip them about an inch into the melted chocolate. Store in an airtight tin for 10 days, or freeze for 2 months.

 **Note**

To add a bit of continental class to this confection, use a bar of European bittersweet chocolate, which is sold in most gourmet shops and even in some supermarkets, in place of the chocolate chips.

HOW TO DIP A FLORENTINE IN CHOCOLATE

Here's the cookie

Here's your hand

BEFORE

Here's the chocolate

Here's the dipped edge

AFTER

Swedish Toast
(Skorporr)

Makes 4 dozen toasts

Sometimes Santa just wants *a nice, comforting goodie to go with his glass of milk: not too sweet, but sweet enough; not too spiced, but spiced enough, like biscotti, only Swedish, and more ethereal. This is it, from one of* Cook & Tell's *Christmas elves. Cardamom is the clue that we're speaking Swedish here.*

1 cup (2 sticks) butter or margarine, softened	3½ cups all-purpose flour
1¼ cups sugar	1 teaspoon baking soda
1 cup sour cream	1 teaspoon salt
2 large eggs	1 teaspoon ground cardamom
	½ teaspoon ground nutmeg

Preheat the oven to 350°F. Grease a 9-by-13-inch baking pan. Cream the butter and sugar in a large bowl. Add the sour cream and eggs and mix well. In a separate medium bowl, combine the flour, baking soda, salt, cardamom, and nutmeg. Add half of the flour mixture to the butter mixture and mix well. Add the remaining flour mixture and mix well. The dough will be sticky. Spread the dough in the prepared pan. Bake for 35 to 40 minutes, or until a tester comes out clean. Cool in the pan on a rack.

When the cake is completely cool, preheat the oven to 325°F.

Cut the cake, in the pan, lengthwise into thirds and then crosswise into ³/₄-inch-wide slices. Lay the slices cut side down on two un-greased cookie sheets and bake until lightly toasted, 15 to 20 minutes. Cool on a rack. Store in a covered jar for 1 week or in the freezer for 1 month.

Holiday Fudge

Makes one 7-by-11-inch or 9-by-13-inch panful

"You probably won't believe this, but I just made the tenth batch this season of the special Holiday Fudge."

— Delphine Snook

For years, **nimble nonagenarian** *Delphine Snook has been using this recipe to please fudge-loving friends and relatives at Christmastime. It's that old recipe from the back of a bag of marshmallows.*

In the spirit of creative tinkering, which Cook & Tell *enthusiastically endorses, Delphine upped the evaporated milk to ³/₄ cup from the original ²/₃ cup, a change she claims makes all the difference in producing a glossy finish. She favors a gentle boil, and the square of unsweetened chocolate is her innovation. Let's give this lady a round of applause!*

4	tablespoons (¹/₂ stick) butter or margarine, plus more for the pan	1	1-ounce square unsweetened chocolate, grated or finely chopped
1¹/₃	cups sugar	1	cup raisins
1¹/₃	cups mini marshmallows	1	cup chopped pecans
³/₄	cup evaporated milk	1	teaspoon orange extract
¹/₄	teaspoon salt	¹/₂	teaspoon almond extract
12	ounces (2 cups) semisweet chocolate chips		

Butter a 7-by-11-inch or 9-by-13-inch baking pan. (The fudge will be thicker in the smaller pan.)

Combine the 4 tablespoons butter, sugar, marshmallows, evaporated milk, and salt in a large saucepan and bring to a boil over medium-high heat. Reduce the heat to medium-low and simmer for 5 minutes, whisking constantly.

Remove from the heat and stir in the chocolate chips and unsweetened chocolate until melted. Stir in the raisins, pecans, orange extract, and almond extract. Beat until glossy, 30 to 60 seconds. Transfer to the prepared pan. Cool and cut into squares.

> ### Note
>
> *After the fudge has cooled, Delphine covers the pan with foil and lets it stand on the counter overnight. She's discovered that she can then tip the fudge out of the pan onto a cutting board for easier cutting with her big chef's knife.*

Keeping Christmas means giving some of it away.

White Chocolate Pretzel Bark

Makes about 2 pounds

Next time you're invited *to a friend's house for dinner, bring a box of this perfectly jolly sweet for a thank-you gift. Or leave bowls of it around the house. When all else fails, just make it some lazy Sunday afternoon and keep the good nibbling to yourself. You don't have to know how to cook to make this lovely, foolproof confection.*

1½ pounds white chocolate (**not** vanilla chips)

½ cup Spanish (skin-on) peanuts

1½ cups broken-up thin pretzels

½ cup dried cherries or dried cranberries

Spray a 10-by-15-inch jelly-roll pan with nonstick cooking spray. Melt the chocolate in the top of a double boiler over simmering water. Remove from the heat and stir in the peanuts, pretzels, and cherries or cranberries. Spread the chocolate mixture in the prepared pan. Let stand at room temperature until hard. Flip the pan over onto a sheet of wax paper to remove the pretzel bark and break it into pieces. Store in a covered tin in the fridge for 2 weeks or in the freezer for 1 month.

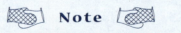 **Note**

Chopped apricots are a good substitute for all or part of the dried cherries or cranberries.

No-Meat Mincemeat

Makes 9 cups

I always thought the "mince" *in mince pie, as we called it, was some kind of dark, mushy, anonymous fruit that came in a jar and was used to make a pie that only your mother and father liked. I grew up and learned not only about the meat, but also how to make a mincemeat filling from real, identifiable fruits for a yummy, meatless pie. Jean Cobb gives us this mincemeat recipe, which she improved on by adding more apples at baking time and substituting a food processor for an old-time grinder.*

3 pounds tart apples, such as Granny Smiths, peeled, cored, and coarsely chopped	1½ cups apple cider
	3 cups packed light brown sugar
1 pound raisins	1½ teaspoons ground cinnamon
1 large orange, peeled, seeded, and cut into chunks	1½ teaspoons ground nutmeg
	1½ teaspoons ground cloves
1 small lemon, peeled, seeded, and cut into chunks	1½ teaspoons salt

Put the apples, raisins, orange, lemon, and cider in a large saucepan and bring to a boil over medium-high heat. Reduce the heat to medium-low and simmer for 15 minutes, stirring occasionally. Add the brown sugar, cinnamon, nutmeg, cloves, and salt and simmer

"The pie I made for my husband, Harrison, with that mincemeat is the first one I ever loved. He loves mince pie, and I never did, so I rarely made it — until I made the mincemeat from COOK & TELL."

— Judy Caner

for 20 to 30 minutes more, or until thick. Pack into three 1-quart air-tight plastic containers and freeze.

When ready to bake a mince pie, defrost one container (3 cups) and mix with 1¹/₂ cups chopped fresh apples.

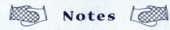

Notes

* *If you can't find apple cider, use 1¹/₂ cups apple juice plus 1 tablespoon vinegar.*

* *A mince pie needs both a top crust and a bottom crust (see Fail-Safe Piecrust, page 311) and should be baked in a preheated 400°F oven for 40 minutes, or until the filling bubbles up through the slits.*

Tips

Cook & Tell promotes tinkering with recipes, and not necessarily *after* you've made it once according to the recipe.

So Barbara Kreuter stepped right up to the pot of simmering mince-meat and added dried cranberries. You don't ask how many, you just add cranberries. Probably a handful.

Executing a trick of her mother-in-law's, Louise Conrad tucked ³/₄ cup orange marmalade and 2 tablespoons margarine into the whole batch of mincemeat. The tinkering even *reads* delicious, doesn't it?

Cranberry Ketchup

Makes about 6 cups

An intriguing change *from the usual cranberry sauce, Chef Fritz Blank's velvety, spicy condiment puts an extra-special highlight on holiday favorites, such as roast turkey, chicken, and pork or baked ham.*

2 pounds fresh cranberries	1 teaspoon ground cloves
3 cups white wine vinegar or cider vinegar	1/2 teaspoon freshly ground white pepper
2 cups sugar	1/2 teaspoon salt
1 tablespoon ground cinnamon	1/4 teaspoon cayenne pepper
1 tablespoon ground ginger	

Put the cranberries and vinegar in a medium nonreactive saucepan and bring to a boil over medium-high heat. Reduce the heat to medium-low and simmer for 8 minutes. Puree the mixture in batches in a blender or food processor. It's very hot; be careful of that "explosion" when you turn on the blender. If using a blender, Fritz recommends replacing the blender lid insert with a short-stemmed funnel, poking down into the blender jar.

Return the puree to the pan over medium-low heat and add the sugar, cinnamon, ginger, cloves, white pepper, salt, and cayenne. Simmer, stirring occasionally, until thick. Cool before ladling into jars or plastic containers. Store in the fridge for up to 3 weeks or in the freezer for up to 3 months.

# Kiwifruit Jam

Makes about 1 cup

Wouldn't it be nice *to be able to make just one perfect jar of lovely jam, when you suddenly remember a friend or a cousin who deserves a homemade remembrance during the holidays, or when your mouth waters for a special topping for your morning muffins? Muriel Lewis found just the recipe in a kiwifruit booklet she picked up in New Zealand. I converted the original microwave directions to conventional stovetop cooking for the old-fashioned pleasure of stirring and watching for the magic, "thick-enough" moment. Those teeny black seeds give a charming little snap to each bite.*

4 kiwifruit, peeled and thinly sliced	1 cup sugar
	½ lemon

Put the kiwifruit, sugar, and the juice of the lemon half in a small saucepan. Cut the lemon rind into four pieces and add. Slowly bring the mixture to a boil over medium heat. Simmer until a teaspoonful placed on a saucer and put in the freezer for 2 minutes thickens to the consistency of jam, about 25 minutes. Remove the lemon rind before pouring the jam into a pretty jar. Store, covered, in the refrigerator for up to 3 weeks.

Note

Those pieces of lemon rind are a yummy reward for the cook to nibble. Enjoy them, all warm and syrupy!

Apricot Marmalade

Makes four ½-pint jars, plus a bit more

Popovers with butter and apricot jam *on Christmas morning are a tradition worth starting, if they're not already one of the things you look forward to on that lovely day. Set a jar of this tawny amber jam on your kitchen windowsill and you'll see the sun shine through, even when it's cloudy.*

1 pound dried apricots	6 tablespoons fresh lemon juice
1½ cups sugar	1 tablespoon grated fresh orange zest
1 tablespoon grated fresh lemon zest	

Soak the apricots overnight in a medium bowl of cold water to barely cover. The next day, put the apricot mixture in a small saucepan and bring to a boil over medium-high heat. Reduce the heat to low and simmer until the apricots are puffy and tender, about 15 minutes. Using a wooden spoon, press the apricots through a sieve into a medium bowl. Don't throw away what doesn't go through the sieve; toss it into the puree. You should have about 2 cups. Put the puree, sugar, lemon zest, lemon juice, and orange zest in a small saucepan over medium heat. Simmer, stirring constantly, until thick and waxy-looking, about 15 minutes. If it starts sticking, reduce the heat. Pour the marmalade into hot, sterilized jars and seal with paraffin or store in the fridge for up to 1 month.

## Chapter 9

HOME IS WHERE THE COOKIES ARE

Born to Bake

Let them eat CAKE

breaking bread

A PIE isn't done 'til it's bubbling

Hot-Tip Corn Bread

Serves 9

All dressed up with a gift jar *of hot pepper jelly and no place to go? Has* Cook & Tell *got a hot tip for you! For the wary but willing, here's a slightly racy corn-bread adventure you can feel free to write home about.*

3 tablespoons butter, plus more for the pan	1 teaspoon baking soda
1 cup all-purpose flour	1 teaspoon baking powder
1 cup yellow cornmeal	1 teaspoon salt
1 tablespoon sugar	½ cup hot pepper jelly
1 tablespoon chili powder	1 cup buttermilk
	2 large eggs, lightly beaten

Preheat the oven to 400°F. Butter an 8- or 9-inch square baking pan.

Combine the flour, cornmeal, sugar, chili powder, baking soda, baking powder, and salt in a large bowl. Melt the 3 tablespoons butter and jelly together in a small saucepan over low heat. Add the jelly mixture, buttermilk, and eggs to the flour mixture and mix just until moistened. Scrape the batter into the prepared pan and bake for 20 minutes, or until the corn bread springs back when gently pressed in the center. Serve hot.

HERE'S A **HOT Tip**

Parsley-Parmesan Biscuits

Makes 16 biscuits

Good news for stews! *Your basic biscuit is given a personality makeover and comes back to life as a mini bread with an attitude. By cutting the dough into squares, you do away with re-rolling the scraps and ending up with a batch that inevitably includes a couple of ugly-duckling specimens. Every good biscuit deserves to be eaten hot (to melt the butter you'll slather on them), so if they're not served straight out of the oven, reheat them in a toaster oven or microwave.*

2½ cups all-purpose flour
1 tablespoon baking powder
1 tablespoon sugar
¼ teaspoon salt
⅓ cup freshly grated Parmesan cheese

⅓ cup vegetable shortening
¼ cup chopped fresh parsley
1 tablespoon snipped fresh chives
1 cup milk

Preheat the oven to 375°F.
Sift 2 cups of the flour, the baking powder, sugar, and salt into a medium bowl. Stir in the cheese. Cut in the shortening with a pastry blender or two knives. Add the parsley and chives. Add the milk all at once and mix with a fork until just combined. The dough will be very wet and soft. Spread ¼ to ½ cup flour onto a work surface and turn

out the dough. Flip it over to take up some flour on both sides. Gently pat the dough into an 8-inch square, $1/2$ inch thick. Cut into 16 squares with a floured chef's knife or a dough scraper. Place the biscuits about 1 inch apart on an ungreased cookie sheet. Bake for 18 minutes, or until golden brown on the bottom and barely colored on top. Serve hot.

Really Easy Yeast Bread
with Herbs and Cheese

Makes one 8-by-5-inch loaf

Our friend Barbara's recipe, *which uses quick-rising yeast, is really fast and easy. If you're spooked about the rising of yeast dough, this is the recipe to help you triumph over timidity. It produces a moist bread with a fine crumb, a great texture, and a savory flavor.*

2 tablespoons (¼ stick) butter, plus more for the pan

2½ cups all-purpose flour

1 cup whole wheat flour

2 tablespoons sugar

1 envelope quick-rising yeast

1 teaspoon salt

½ cup milk

1 large egg, at room temperature

¾ cup grated sharp cheddar cheese (about 3 ounces)

2 tablespoons snipped fresh chives

2 teaspoons chopped fresh thyme or 1 teaspoon dried

1 teaspoon freshly ground black pepper

Butter an 8-by-5-inch loaf pan. Combine the all-purpose and whole wheat flours in a large bowl; reserve 1 cup and set aside. Add the sugar, yeast, and salt to the remaining flour in the bowl. Heat ½ cup water, the milk, and 2 tablespoons butter to 125° to 130°F in a small saucepan. Stir into the flour mixture. Stir in the egg, cheese, chives, thyme, and pepper. Add just enough of the reserved flour to make a soft dough. Knead on a floured

ALL RISE!

surface for 5 minutes, or until smooth and no longer sticky. Shape the dough into a loaf and put it in the prepared pan.

Preheat the oven to 400°F. Fill a 9-by-13-inch baking pan halfway with boiling water. Put a wire rack over the pan of water and set the bread pan on the rack. Cover loosely with a dishtowel. Let rise for 25 minutes, or until almost doubled. Put the pan of water on the bottom rack of the oven and the bread pan on a rack above it. Bake for 20 minutes, or until the bread sounds hollow when thumped on the bottom. Cool completely before slicing and serving.

All Rise! (In a Warm Place)

My latest "warm place" for helping bread dough rise involves preheating the oven to "warm" or its absolute lowest setting, then turning it off and putting a 9-by-13-inch baking pan full of hot tap water on the lowest rack. Put the bowl of dough on the rack above and close the oven door. If your lowest oven temperature seems too hot for comfort, leave the door open for a minute after turning off the oven, then stash the pan of water and the bowl of dough inside.

If, like April Maron, you live in a drafty, old Victorian house, your need for a warm place for bread rising is acute. If you count a newfangled microwave oven among your cherished kitchen collectibles, escape the draft her way: Boil some water in a bowl in the microwave, remove it, and send in the bowl of dough. *Don't* turn on the microwave again. It will stay nice and warm in there while your dough rises.

Maple-Oat Muffins with Crumble Topping

Makes 8 muffins

When the sap is running *in New England, we like to pay homage by pointing cooking endeavors in a maple direction. But a jug of Grade B Dark syrup is always on hand for waffles (page 155), salad dressing (page 59), and these mighty muffins, which began life in a recipe Gerry Connors sent from a Canadian cookbook,* Let's Bake Bread. *I gave it a tune-up and endowed it with a cozy crumble topping.*

4 tablespoons (½ stick) butter or margarine, softened, plus more for the tin (optional)

½ cup sugar

½ teaspoon salt

1¼ cups all-purpose flour

2 teaspoons baking powder

¾ cup old-fashioned or quick-cooking rolled oats

½ cup milk

½ cup pure maple syrup

Crumble Topping (recipe follows)

Preheat the oven to 350°F. Butter a muffin tin or line the cups with paper liners.

Cream the 4 tablespoons butter, sugar, and salt in a medium bowl. Combine the flour and baking powder in a small bowl and, using a pastry blender or two knives, cut it into the butter mixture until crumbly. Stir in the oats. Combine the milk and maple syrup in a small bowl and stir into the oat mixture until just moistened. Fill the muffin cups three-quarters full with the batter. Sprinkle each muffin with a spoonful of the Crumble Topping. Bake for 25 minutes, or until a toothpick probe comes out clean. Cool in the pan on a wire rack for 10 minutes. Serve warm or at room temperature.

Crumble Topping

1½ tablespoons all-purpose flour

1½ tablespoons sugar

1 teaspoon butter, softened

1 tablespoon old-fashioned or quick-cooking rolled oats

1 tablespoon finely chopped pecans

Using a fork, combine the flour, sugar, and butter in a small bowl. Stir in the oats and pecans.

Welsh Cakes

Makes 60 cakes

The British observe St. David's Day *on March 1. To cele-brate the special day of the patron saint of Wales, they make these sconelike cakes. They're sweet, like cookies; more substantial, like biscuits, but better. You need to stick around while the cakes cook, because they have to be turned, but they're worth it.*

8 tablespoons (1 stick) butter	1 teaspoon ground nutmeg
½ cup vegetable shortening	1 teaspoon salt
1 cup sugar	1 cup dried currants
3⅓ cups all-purpose flour	1 large egg
1½ teaspoons baking powder	½ cup milk
½ teaspoon baking soda	

Preheat an electric skillet or griddle to 250°F.

Using an electric mixer, cream the butter, shortening, and sugar in a large bowl. Sift the flour, baking powder, baking soda, nutmeg, and salt into a medium bowl and mix into the butter mixture with an electric mixer on low speed. Add the currants. Using a fork, lightly beat the egg

---

✦ Note ✦

Place as many cakes in your electric skillet or griddle as will fit, allowing room for turning. I can bake 22 at a time in my skillet. If you use a regular skillet or griddle on the stovetop, you must keep watch over the heat, keeping it low enough to avoid overbrowning.

and milk in a small bowl and mix it into the flour mixture. The dough will be soft.

Pat the dough flat on a floured surface with floured hands. Roll the dough out 1/3 inch thick. Cut into 2-inch rounds with a biscuit cutter.

Cook in batches on the skillet or griddle, turning at least twice, for 10 to 12 minutes, or until golden brown. Cool on a rack. Serve.

Irish Oat Scones

Makes 1 dozen scones

"Split the scone, butter it, spread it with jam and clotted cream, in that order, and put the top back on."

— Enid Farmer, Englishwoman

I don't care how you pronounce "scones." *All that matters is a good recipe, a light touch, and serving them hot out of the oven. Joanne Jensen sent in this terrific recipe printed on the back of a St. Patrick's Day greeting card. Put the teakettle on and call the kitty! Time to snuggle up with the comforts of cat, cup, and scone.*

2½ cups all-purpose flour
¼ cup old-fashioned or quick-cooking rolled oats
2 tablespoons sugar
1 teaspoon baking soda
1 teaspoon cream of tartar
½ teaspoon salt

4 tablespoons (½ stick) butter, cut into pieces
½ cup golden raisins
1 cup buttermilk

Butter, jam, or honey

Preheat the oven to 400°F.
  Combine the flour, oats, sugar, baking soda, cream of tartar, and salt in a large bowl. Using a pastry blender or two knives, cut in the butter until the mixture looks like coarse crumbs. Add the raisins and toss. Add the buttermilk and, using a fork, toss lightly until just moistened. Gather up the dough and turn it onto a floured surface. Pat it out about ¾ inch thick. Cut into 2-inch circles with a floured biscuit cutter or a glass. Gather the scraps, re-roll, and cut more. Or avoid re-rolling by dividing the dough in half, patting each into a ¾-inch-thick disk, and cutting each disk into six wedges. Bake on an ungreased cookie sheet for 10 to 15 minutes, or until golden. Serve hot with butter, jam, or honey.

Tea Brack (Irish Tea Bread)

Makes two 8-by-5-inch loaves

"I always make four to six loaves *of tea brack for the holidays,"* wrote Gerry Connors, enclosing this "real Irish recipe" given to him by Sheila Patterson. She's from County Monaghan, where the relevant holiday for traditional tea brack is Halloween; Gerry makes it at Christmastime. He's been thinking of adding nuts, but according to friends and family, he says, "this would be some kind of heresy."

- 1 15-ounce package raisins (about 3 cups)
- 1 1-pound package dark brown sugar
- 2½ cups brewed tea (any kind will do), cooled
- 2 large eggs, lightly beaten

- ½ teaspoon ground nutmeg
- ½ teaspoon ground allspice
- ½ teaspoon ground cinnamon
- 4 cups self-rising flour (see Note)

Butter, cream cheese, or marmalade

Combine the raisins and brown sugar in a large bowl. Add the tea, cover, and let stand at room temperature overnight.

Preheat the oven to 350°F. Grease and flour two 8-by-5-inch loaf pans.

Add the eggs, nutmeg, allspice, and cinnamon to the raisin mixture. Stir in the self-rising flour. Pour the batter into the prepared pans. Bake for 45 to 60 minutes, or until a tester stuck into the center of a loaf comes out clean. Cool for 5 minutes in the pans on a rack, then turn out to cool completely on the rack. Slice and serve spread with butter or cream cheese. It's also lovely toasted, buttered, and anointed with marmalade.

 **Note**

To turn 4 cups all-purpose flour into 4 cups self-rising flour, add 2 tablespoons baking powder and 2 teaspoons salt to the flour and sift before adding to the batter.

There is always time for tea.

Fail-Safe Piecrust

Makes enough for 3 double-crust or 6 single-crust pies

Here it is: the one — the only — *way to make piecrust, as far as I'm concerned. This pastry is easy to mix and roll out, it's simultaneously flaky and tender, and it has revolutionized the baking lives of at least two of my friends. The husband of one of them even thanked me personally. You can freeze the unbaked pastry disks. I always feel so rich with my six nascent crusts (sometimes seven, if I push it) in the freezer. The only downside is the feeling of loss when they're all gone.*

2½ cups vegetable shortening	1 tablespoon salt
6 cups all-purpose flour	1 large egg
1 tablespoon sugar	2 tablespoons white vinegar

Put the shortening in a large bowl and dump in the flour, sugar, and salt, in that order. Using a pastry blender or two knives, cut the shortening into the dry ingredients. Beat the egg in a measuring cup with a spout, stir in the vinegar, and add water to equal 1 cup. Gradually drizzle the egg mixture into the flour mixture, tossing with a fork, drizzling more of the egg mixture over undampened places, and then tossing again, until the pastry gathers into a mass. Divide the pastry into six portions and quickly form each into a disk. Put each disk into a zipper-lock plastic bag and store in the freezer.

> ### Note
>
> *Freshly made, a disk of dough should be chilled for about 3 hours before rolling out. A frozen one must be thoroughly defrosted before being rolled out.*

Cranberry-Raisin Pie

Serves 6 to 8

Ferdie Plante ran a seasonal art gallery *over in the Harbor for years and would occasionally lure me in to talk cooking. One August, I left the "e" off his last name when I printed one of his recipes in the newsletter. By the end of the season, he'd gotten over it and began telling me about his favorite pie, but he agreed to hand over the recipe only if I would promise to spell his name correctly.*

³⁄₄ cup sugar, plus more to
    sprinkle on the crust
1 tablespoon cornstarch
³⁄₄ cup light corn syrup
2 tablespoons grated fresh
    orange zest
3 cups fresh cranberries

¹⁄₂ cup golden raisins
¹⁄₂ cup finely chopped walnuts
2 tablespoons (¹⁄₄ stick) butter
   Pastry for a double-crust
    9-inch pie (see Fail-Safe
    Piecrust, page 311)

Milk, for brushing the crust

Combine the ³⁄₄ cup sugar and cornstarch in a large saucepan and mix well. Stir in the corn syrup, ¹⁄₂ cup water, and the orange zest and bring to a boil over medium heat. Stir in the cranberries, raisins, and walnuts. Reduce the heat to low, cover, and simmer until the cranberries pop, 3 to 5 minutes. Remove the pan from the heat and add the butter, but do not stir. Cool.

Preheat the oven to 425°F.

Roll out one crust and line a pie plate. Trim, leaving a ¹⁄₂-inch overhang. Fill with the cranberry mixture. Roll out the top crust, cut vents, and fit it on the pie. Seal and crimp the edges. Brush the top with milk and sprinkle with sugar. Bake for 40 to 50 minutes, or until the crust is golden brown and juice bubbles out of the pastry vents. Serve warm or at room temperature.

> ### Note
>
> *Alternatively, a lattice crust is a lovely way to let the glistening filling show through.*

Be patient.

The pie isn't done until it's bubbling.

Grandma Schmidt's Apple Pie

Serves 6

Other people have their *lawyers and accountants. I have my upholsterer, and he had his mother, Grandma Schmidt, and she had her apple pie. This is it. The combination of apple varieties and the old-fashioned crust recipe, originally devised by Crisco, distinguish this from any other apple pie I have ever made. I honor Grandma's memory by setting aside my own favorite Fail-Safe Piecrust (page 311) and using her recipe when I make apple pie. It's an ensemble!*

Crust

2¼ cups sifted all-purpose flour

1 teaspoon salt

¾ cup vegetable shortening

Filling

6–7 apples, peeled, cored, and thinly sliced (this is a nice mix: 1 Red Delicious, 1 Braeburn, 3 McIntoshes, 1 Granny Smith)

1 cup sugar

1 tablespoon all-purpose flour

½ teaspoon ground cinnamon

Scant ¼ teaspoon ground nutmeg

1 tablespoon butter

Milk

1 tablespoon sugar mixed with ¼ teaspoon ground cinnamon

Preheat the oven to 475°F.

To make the crust: Sift the flour and salt into a large bowl. Put ⅓ cup of the flour mixture into a small bowl and stir in ¼ cup water;

set aside. Cut the shortening into the remaining flour mixture in the large bowl until pea-size lumps form. Add the flour-and-water paste and, using your hands, toss lightly just until it holds together. Divide the pastry into two portions. Roll out one crust and line a pie plate. Trim, leaving a ½-inch overhang.

To make the filling: Mound the sliced apples in the pastry-lined pie plate. Combine the sugar, flour, cinnamon, and nutmeg in a small bowl and pour over and between the apple slices, gently shaking the pie plate to let the sugar mixture sift down. Dot with the butter.

To assemble: Roll out the top crust, cut vents, and fit it on the pie. Seal and crimp the edges. Brush the top with milk and sprinkle with the cinnamon sugar. Bake for 5 minutes. Reduce the oven temperature to 375°F and bake for 45 minutes more, or until juice bubbles out of the pastry vents. Serve warm or at room temperature.

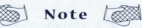

Note

Place a very thin layer of oh-so-thinly-sliced cheddar cheese on the bottom crust of the pie before filling with sliced apples. A cheese shaver will do a swell job.

Anne's Best Apple Tart

Serves 6

An old friend gave me this *recipe when we lived in adjoining "half-houses" in the historic district of Annapolis. I've always made it in a 9- or 10-inch cast-iron skillet, and I've never served it upside down (apples up), à la tarte tatin, the way I think she said to. I just love the look of the rich crust on top and the lemony, brown-sugary surprise you find underneath when you dig in.*

8 tablespoons (1 stick) butter

1 cup packed light brown sugar

3 cups peeled, cored, and thinly sliced apples

2 teaspoons grated fresh lemon zest

2 teaspoons fresh lemon juice

¼ teaspoon ground cinnamon

Crust

1¼ cups all-purpose flour

2 teaspoons grated fresh lemon zest

1 teaspoon sugar

8 tablespoons (1 stick) butter, cut into 8 pieces, chilled

1 large egg, lightly beaten

Preheat the oven to 450°F.

Melt the butter in a 9- or 10-inch cast-iron skillet, or an equivalent flameproof pan or pie plate, over medium heat. Add the brown sugar and cook for 3 minutes, or until the sugar dissolves. Cool slightly. Spread the apples over the butter mixture and sprinkle with the lemon zest, lemon juice, and cinnamon. Set aside.

To make the crust: Combine the flour, lemon zest, and sugar in a medium bowl. Using a pastry blender or two knives, cut the butter into the flour mixture. Using a fork, work in the egg until the pastry is well blended and holds together. Form the pastry into a disk. Roll out the pastry between two sheets of wax paper to fit over the pan of apples, with a little extra to bunch up around the edges. Cover the apples with the pastry. Paste bits of pastry here and there, if necessary, to make it fit tightly to the side of the skillet, pushing the edges gently into a thicker rim. Bake for 35 to 45 minutes, or until the top is golden brown and syrup is oozing out along the edges. Serve warm.

Maple Egg Tarts

Makes six 2³/₄-inch tarts

In homage to the maple syrup season, *I converted an old Nova Scotian recipe, with its brown sugar and vinegar, into a lus-cious, maple-flavored dainty, sparked with lemon juice. Egg tarts come in myriad versions all across Canada, and maple syrup is not exactly unknown up there, so I wouldn't be surprised to learn that some Saskatchewanian or Québecois has already thought of this win-ning combination. The filling is soft, almost runny, and just lovely.*

Pastry for a single-crust 9- or
   10-inch pie (see Fail-Safe
   Piecrust, page 311)
1 large egg

¹/₂ cup packed light brown sugar
¹/₂ cup pure maple syrup
2 teaspoons fresh lemon juice
1 teaspoon vanilla extract

Preheat the oven to 400°F.
Cut the pastry in rounds to fit six 2³/₄-inch muffin cups and press them gently into place.

Beat the egg in a medium bowl until light-colored. Beat in the brown sugar, maple syrup, lemon juice, and vanilla. Fill the unbaked shells a little more than halfway. Bake for 5 minutes, reduce the oven temperature to 350°F, and bake for 10 minutes more, or until the crust is lightly browned and the filling is a somewhat translucent dark amber. Cool in the pan on a rack and serve.

Shirley Peasley's Pumpkin Pie

Serves 6

You can always justify *a piece of pumpkin pie: It's a vegetable!*
Shirley's version of the fundamental fall dessert floats above the rest,
practically pumped up into a soufflé with beaten egg whites. And
mind those eggs. They're extra large, a departure from the usual
large ones.

2 **extra-large** eggs, separated, at room temperature	½ teaspoon ground ginger
1 1-pound can pumpkin (1½ cups)	½ teaspoon ground nutmeg
	½ teaspoon salt
1 cup sugar	1¼ cups milk
1½ tablespoons all-purpose flour	Pastry for a single-crust 9- or 10-inch pie (see Fail-Safe
½ teaspoon ground cinnamon	Piecrust, page 311)

Preheat the oven to 350°F.
Using an electric mixer, beat the egg whites in a medium bowl until stiff. Set aside. Using clean beaters, lightly beat the egg yolks in a large bowl. Add the pumpkin, sugar, flour, cinnamon, ginger, nutmeg, salt, and milk and beat well. Fold in the beaten egg whites.

Roll out the crust and line a pie plate. Trim, leaving a ½-inch overhang. Fold in the edge of the crust and crimp. Pour in the pumpkin mixture. Bake for 1 hour, or until set in the center. (It will continue to cook as it cools. The filling puffs up at first, then shrinks slightly.) Cool and serve.

Fresh Strawberry Tart

Serves 6 to 8

Native berries sparkle brightly *in Sally Bobbitt's essence-of-summer tart. But strawberry season isn't very long, and don't you just want summer to last forever? That's when those all-season mutants, as big and firm as they are, come in handy and do the job surprisingly well.*

Crust

- 12 tablespoons (1½ sticks) butter, softened
- 2 large egg yolks
- ½ teaspoon vanilla extract
- ½ cup sugar
- ¼ teaspoon salt
- 2 cups all-purpose flour
  Grated zest of 1 lemon

Filling

- 1 10-ounce jar red currant jelly
- 5 tablespoons sugar
- 2 envelopes unflavored gelatin
- 1½ pints (3 cups) fresh strawberries, rinsed, hulled, and halved or quartered if large

To make the crust: Using a wooden spoon, combine the butter, egg yolks, vanilla, sugar, and salt in a medium bowl. Work in the flour and lemon zest with the spoon or your fingers. Gently knead the dough just until it holds together. Form into two disks, wrap in plastic wrap, and chill until firm enough to roll out, about 1 hour. (This is enough dough for two tart shells; you can freeze the unused half for your next tart. Thaw before rolling out.)

Preheat the oven to 450°F.

Roll out half of the pastry between two sheets of wax paper, about ¼ inch thick—not as thin as for a standard piecrust. Line a tart or quiche pan with the crust, then line the crust with wax paper and weigh it down with a layer of uncooked beans or pie weights; or use Auntie's Cracker Method (see below). Bake until golden, about 15 minutes. Check after 5 minutes and reduce the oven temperature to 400°F if the sides begin to brown before the bottom. Cool before removing the wax paper and weights.

To make the filling: Combine the jelly, sugar, and gelatin in a medium saucepan and bring to a boil over medium beat, stirring to completely dissolve the gelatin. Remove from the heat and gently stir in the berries. Pour the filling into the baked crust. Chill until firm, about 6 hours. Serve cold.

Auntie's Cracker Method

To bake a pie shell that will be filled later, Auntie lined it with crackers. She stood them up gently all around the edge and laid them flat on the bottom. She used saltines or Ritz crackers. I use saltines (it takes about seventeen) and it works like magic. No puffing pastry, no sagging sides, and no mess of beans or weights to fish out when the crust is baked. Just remember to remove the crackers before filling the baked crust.

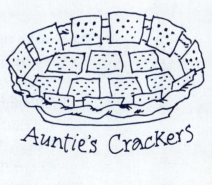

Auntie's Crackers

Rhubarb-Cherry Crisp

Serves 6

When rhubarb season rolls around, *we get another chance to prove to ourselves that it's impossible to OD on what home-makers of bygone days called "pie plant." We stew it; we make pies, cakes, and crumbles; and sometimes we just throw together this simple crisp.*

4 tablespoons (½ stick) butter, plus more for the casserole dish

2 cups graham-cracker crumbs (about 10 graham crackers; see Note)

¾ cup packed light brown sugar

½ teaspoon ground cinnamon

¾ pound rhubarb, cut into 1-inch lengths

1 cup dried cherries

⅓ cup orange juice

Vanilla ice cream

Preheat the oven to 350°F. Butter a 1½-quart casserole dish. Combine the 4 tablespoons butter and graham-cracker crumbs in a medium bowl. Pile—don't pack—half of the crumb mixture into the casserole dish. Combine the brown sugar and cinnamon in a large bowl; reserve 1 tablespoon for the topping. Add the rhubarb, cherries, and orange juice to the brown-sugar mixture in the large bowl and toss to mix. Dump the fruit mixture into the casserole dish and top with the remaining crumb mixture. Sprinkle the reserved sugar mixture over the top. Cover loosely with foil. Bake for 20 minutes. Remove the foil and bake for 30 minutes more, or until the rhubarb is tender and the crumbs are lightly browned. Serve warm with vanilla ice cream.

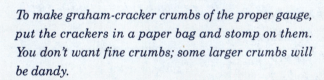

Note

To make graham-cracker crumbs of the proper gauge, put the crackers in a paper bag and stomp on them. You don't want fine crumbs; some larger crumbs will be dandy.

Hot-Water Sponge Cake

Serves 8 to 10

*"I really, **really** love to bake cakes. My mother let me make a cake when I was very young, and I've been hooked ever since. Sometimes I just have to bake a cake."*

— Jo McGruder

Laura White and two of her friends *decided it wasn't fair to have to bake one's own birthday cake, "so Georgia made my cake, June made Georgia's, and I made June's," wrote Laura. "It was always the Hot-Water Sponge. It has continued to be the birthday cake for the whole White family." The soft and the tender meet right here, in one wonderfully light cake with a melting, delicate crumb.*

4 large eggs, separated, at room temperature	¼ teaspoon salt
	1 teaspoon lemon extract
1½ cups sugar	
1½ cups all-purpose flour	Confectioners' sugar
1 teaspoon baking powder	Fresh berries

Preheat the oven to 325°F.

Using an electric mixer, beat the egg whites in a medium bowl until glossy and stiff but not dry. Set aside in the fridge. Using clean beaters, beat the egg yolks in a large bowl until light-colored. Beat in the sugar, 1 tablespoon at a time, until very thick. Beat in ½ cup boiling water. Sift the flour, baking powder, and salt into a medium bowl and stir into the egg mixture by hand. Stir in the lemon extract. Gently fold in the beaten egg whites. Pour the batter into an ungreased 10-inch tube pan. Bake for 1 hour, or until a tester stuck in the center comes out clean and the cake begins to shrink from the sides of the pan and springs back when lightly touched. Turn the pan upside down to cool, setting it on three or four cups or an inverted funnel. When cool, run a knife around the edge of the pan and slap the bottom, if necessary, to release the cake. Sift confectioners' sugar over the cake, top with fresh berries, and serve.

Sticky Gingerbread

Makes two 8- or 9-inch square cakes

On one of our visits to England, *we stayed in the home of members of the parish church that was sponsoring the "holiday." When we returned from our daily jaunts into Wiltshire, our hostess always served us afternoon tea and cakes. Her moist, dark gingerbread, called "Hurry-Up Gingerbread" in a cookery booklet of American sweets sold at the American Museum in Bath, England, is actually quite British in its "stickiness." So I renamed it, to put its lovely texture right up front. The cream topping is Gene Simmons's idea; no respectable Brit would dream of faking his beloved and ever available double Devon cream.*

8 tablespoons (1 stick) butter, softened, plus more for the pans
1 cup sugar
2 cups molasses
1 large egg
3 cups all-purpose flour
2 teaspoons ground ginger
1 teaspoon baking soda

1 teaspoon ground cinnamon
1 teaspoon salt
¹/₂ teaspoon ground nutmeg
1¹/₄ cups milk

Mock Devonshire Cream (recipe follows)
Raspberry jam to gild the lily

Preheat the oven to 325°F. Lightly butter two 8- or 9-inch square baking pans, line them with wax paper, and lightly butter the wax paper.

Cream the 8 tablespoons butter and sugar in a large bowl. Beat in the molasses and egg. Sift the flour, ginger, baking soda, cinnamon, salt, and nutmeg in a medium bowl. Add gradually to the molasses mixture, blending well. Add the milk and mix thoroughly. Pour the batter into the prepared pans and bake for 50 minutes, or until a tester stuck in the center of a cake brings up sticky crumbs, not goo. Turn the cakes out of the pans onto racks and immediately and carefully peel off the wax paper. When cool, invert onto a cookie sheet or

Note

Since the batter is heavy, the cake bakes with a characteristic "slump" in the middle. When the cakes are cut into bars or squares, this feature is immaterial and in no way detracts from their sticky goodness.

breadboard and cut into small bars or larger squares with a sharp knife or a dough scraper. Serve with a dollop of Mock Devonshire Cream and a dab of raspberry jam.

Mock Devonshire Cream

4 ounces cream cheese, at room temperature
1 teaspoon confectioners' sugar

1 cup heavy cream
¼ teaspoon vanilla extract

Whir the cream cheese, confectioners' sugar, cream, and vanilla in a food processor until the consistency resembles thick mayonnaise or soft-serve ice cream. (Alternatively, using an electric mixer, beat together all the ingredients in a medium bowl.) Store, covered, in the fridge.

In the dearest baking story I have ever heard, a woman made gingerbread every full moon for her husband of fifty years.

"The moon is so bright and beautiful in Canada and the moon path across the water just outstanding," she wrote. "One evening when my husband's aunt and I were there alone, she decided to bake gingerbread. We sat in 'the light of the moon' to eat the warm cake," which, she added, "was the only way to eat gingerbread."

"This was years ago, when my husband was still working and flying to Canada on weekends. But gingerbread by the light of the moon became a tradition of our own. We have no special recipe, but like it with a warm lemon sauce, a lemon glaze, or upside down with butter, brown sugar, and peaches or apricots."

Sounds like a special recipe to me. There's a secret ingredient in there, too, available free to every starry-eyed baker and her gingerbread buddy on the planet. It's what makes the world go round.

Nobby Apple Cake with Rosemary Butterscotch Sauce

Serves 9

Here's why I like this simple country cake. *It's not an elaborate production. You just eat it and love it. Nutmeg only, no cinnamon, really brings out its appl-itude and makes it interesting and wonderful. Also, it was my mum's recipe, except for the sauce, and it has a cute name. End of discussion.*

2   tablespoons vegetable short-
    ening, plus more for the pan
1   cup sugar
1   large egg
2   large apples, peeled, cored,
    and diced (about 3 cups;
    Cortlands are good)
¼   cup chopped walnuts

1   teaspoon vanilla extract
1   cup all-purpose flour
1   teaspoon baking soda
½   teaspoon ground nutmeg
½   teaspoon salt

Rosemary Butterscotch Sauce
   (recipe follows)

Preheat the oven to 350°F. Grease an 8-inch square baking pan. Cream the 2 tablespoons shortening and sugar in a medium bowl. Add the egg and mix well. Stir in the apples, walnuts, and vanilla. Sift the flour, baking soda, nutmeg, and salt into a large bowl and stir into the apple mixture. Turn the batter into the prepared pan. Bake for 35 minutes, or until the cake springs back when gently pressed. Serve warm or cold with the Rosemary Butterscotch Sauce.

Rosemary Butterscotch Sauce

To crown this everyday cake *with the kind of splendor my mother would have considered unnecessary, you need a sauce like this to pour over each helping.*

½ cup half-and-half

3 tablespoons butter

½ cup granulated sugar, plus a pinch

⅓ cup packed light brown sugar

2 2-inch sprigs fresh rosemary

Combine the half-and-half, butter, ½ cup granulated sugar, and brown sugar in a small saucepan over medium heat. Cook, stirring often, until as thick as desired—6 to 8 minutes for medium drippiness.

Meanwhile, snip the leaves off the rosemary sprigs and grind them with the pinch of sugar with a mortar and pestle, or bruise them with the sugar with a wooden spoon in a wooden bowl. Add the rosemary mixture to the sauce toward the end of the cooking time. Remove from the heat and let stand for 5 minutes. Serve warm with the cake.

 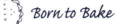

Sugar Crispies

Makes 3 to 4 dozen cookies

For the yeast-fearing, *here's the perfect recipe. There's no waiting for the dough to rise, so there's no wondering if the dough has risen enough. And as an added attraction, each cookie comes equipped with the unique (really!) delicate flavor of yeast, as well as a flaky texture unattainable in any other way. Delight your family! Amaze your friends! Sneak a handful for yourself!*

1 cup (2 sticks) butter or margarine, softened, plus more for the cookie sheet

1 envelope active dry yeast

2 cups all-purpose flour

1 cup sugar, plus more if needed

Preheat the oven to 375°F. Butter a cookie sheet well.
Dissolve the yeast in ⅓ cup warm (about 105°F) water in a small bowl. Cream the 1 cup butter in a medium bowl. Using a wooden spoon, stir in the flour, then work in the yeast mixture. The dough will be soft. Put the sugar on a plate. Form walnut-size pieces of dough roughly into balls and roll the balls in the sugar. Flatten each ball with the heel of your hand, right in the plate of sugar. Turn over and use three fingers to flatten each some more. This ensures that the cookies take up enough sugar to bake up crispy. Using a spatula, transfer the floppy circles of sugared dough to the cookie sheet. Bake for 15 minutes, or until golden but not browned. Watch carefully so they don't burn. Cool on a rack. Store in an airtight tin for up to 1 week.

Extraordinary Butter Cookies

Makes 4 to 5 dozen cookies

We got our orders from Elfrieda Palmer: *"Find baker's ammonia," the lady said. "It makes great and flaky cookies." She and her sister had exhausted all their possible sources and come up empty.*

After a series of fruitless, clandestine rendezvous with a few pharmacists, we finally located the stuff right under our nose (and, oh my, what a smell!) at the local drugstore. (Luckily, its strong odor disappears during baking.) It sure makes the most delicate cookies, so ethereal they practically self-destruct.

1 cup (2 sticks) butter, softened	**Topping**
1 cup sugar	1 large egg
1 large egg	1 tablespoon sugar
1 teaspoon baker's ammonia (see Note)	1 tablespoon ground unblanched almonds
3 cups sifted all-purpose flour	

Preheat the oven to 350°F.

Cream the butter and sugar in a large bowl. Add the egg and mix well. Pulverize the baker's ammonia, using the back of a spoon in a wooden bowl or a mortar and pestle. Add the baker's ammonia and flour to the butter mixture and work the dough until you can pack it into a ball. Roll out the dough thinly, using little or no additional flour. Using cookie cutters, cut into rounds or other shapes and place on ungreased cookie sheets.

To make the topping: Beat the egg in a small bowl. Combine the sugar and almonds in a separate small bowl.

Using the back of a teaspoon, spread a portion of the beaten egg on each cookie. Carefully sprinkle the sugar mixture over the egg in the middle third of each cookie. Bake for 8 to 10 minutes, or until pale golden, watching carefully. Hold your breath if you open the oven door while the cookies are baking. The smell goes away when they're done. Cool on a rack. Store in an airtight tin for up to 3 weeks.

 **Note**

If your local drugstore doesn't carry baker's ammonia, it is also available from The Baker's Catalog *from King Arthur Flour in Vermont. Call 1-800-827-6836.*

Mrs. Russell's Oatmeal-Raisin Cookies

Makes 5 dozen cookies

Back in the eighties, *the First Lady's press secretary invited all the staff members to bring two dozen homemade cookies to their boss's birthday party. Staring in disbelief at her deputy's contribution to the shindig, the secretary moaned, "Just crumbs. Total humiliation." We know that story was true: We read it in the paper.*

Anyway, aware that something was terribly wrong at the White House (and we're not talking politics here), Cook & Tell *invited readers to submit their nominations for National Cookie, in a contest that was to last one year. After tedious testing, shrouded in secrecy, in undisclosed locations all over America, Jane Jentsch's cookie won First Cookie!*

P.S. There really was a Mrs. Russell. She was Jane's best friend's neighbor.

1 cup vegetable shortening	1 teaspoon baking soda
1 cup packed dark brown sugar	1 teaspoon salt
1 cup granulated sugar	1/2 teaspoon baking powder
1/2 cup molasses	2 cups old-fashioned or quick-cooking rolled oats
2 large eggs	
2 teaspoons vanilla extract	1 cup raisins
2 cups all-purpose flour	1 cup chopped walnuts
1 1/2 teaspoons ground cinnamon	

FIRST COOKIE

Preheat the oven to 325°F.

Cream the shortening, brown sugar, and granulated sugar in a large bowl. Beat in the molasses, eggs, and vanilla. Sift the flour, cinnamon, baking soda, salt, and baking powder into a medium bowl. Stir into the sugar mixture. Fold in the oats, raisins, and walnuts. Let stand in the fridge, covered, for at least 1 hour or overnight. Drop by heaping tablespoon onto an ungreased cookie sheet and press down lightly to flatten. Bake for 13 minutes, or until lightly browned. Let the cookies stand for 30 seconds on the cookie sheet before transferring them to a rack. Cool. Store in an airtight tin for up to 1 week.

 **Note**

For special occasions, such as the next time you make cookies, you can jazz them up with such additives as dried cranberries or cherries, chopped crystallized ginger, or chopped dried apricots.

Apricot-Orange Oatmeal Cookies

Makes about 4 dozen cookies

A cookie recipe that tells you *right up front where it's coming from has me reaching for mixing bowl and wooden spoon before I've read through the recipe. I'm a pushover for a good oatmeal cookie, and the added fruity attractions and a haunting trace of cardamom in Maggie Rogers's softly chewy version of the classic make it a shoo-in for our scrapbook of all-time favorites.*

1 cup dried apricots, finely diced	1¼ cups all-purpose flour
⅓ cup butter, plus more for the cookie sheet	½ teaspoon baking soda
⅓ cup vegetable shortening	½ teaspoon ground cinnamon
1 cup packed light brown sugar	½ teaspoon ground cardamom
⅓ cup granulated sugar	½ teaspoon salt
1 large egg	2¼ cups old-fashioned rolled oats
1 teaspoon vanilla extract	48–50 pecan halves (1 for each cookie)
1 tablespoon grated fresh orange zest	

Soak the apricots in ½ cup boiling water in a small bowl while preparing the dough. Preheat the oven to 350°F. Butter a cookie sheet.

Cream the ⅓ cup butter, shortening, brown sugar, and granulated sugar in a large bowl. Add the egg, vanilla, and orange zest and mix well. Sift the flour, baking soda, cinnamon, cardamom, and salt into a medium bowl. Stir into the sugar mixture. Drain the apricots and add them and the oats. Stir. And stir. And *stir!* Drop by teaspoons onto the prepared cookie sheet. Press a pecan half onto each cookie. Bake for 12 to 15 minutes, or until the edges are only lightly browned. Let the cookies cool on the cookie sheet for 2 minutes before transferring them to a rack. Cool. Store in airtight tins for up to 1 week.

Argo Molasses Cookies

Makes 4 dozen cookies

When our neighbors Marj and Eliot *ran the* Argo *excursion boat out of the Harbor, they sometimes offered their passengers these molasses cookies, baked for them by another mutual neighbor, Marge Collins. The classic molasses flavor, the chewy-unto-crunchiness, the almost perfect roundness, and the intriguing crackly top make me want to say cookies don't come any better than these. Except my files bulge with great cookie recipes . . . and the next great cookie always comes along. But these—oh, these are good!*

1½	cups vegetable shortening	4	teaspoons baking soda
2½	cups sugar	2	teaspoons ground cinnamon
½	cup molasses	2	teaspoons ground ginger
2	large eggs	2	teaspoons ground cloves
4	cups all-purpose flour	1	teaspoon salt

Preheat the oven to 375°F.

Cream the shortening and 2 cups of the sugar in a large bowl. Beat in the molasses and eggs. Sift the flour, baking soda, cinnamon, ginger, cloves, and salt into a separate large bowl. Stir into the sugar mixture, mixing thoroughly; do not beat. Form the dough into 1-inch balls and roll the balls in the remaining ½ cup sugar on a plate. Place on ungreased cookie sheets 2 inches apart and bake for 12 minutes, or until "crackled" and set, but still somewhat soft. Cool on a rack. Store in an airtight tin for up to 1 week.

Mama's Blondies

Makes 16 blondies

Betty Wilton fondly remembers *her mother's simple squares. Although she has seen several similar recipes, she says, like a loyal daughter, "I'll stick to this one." It's one of those purely predictable recipes you used to practically make in your sleep and you always loved but lost track of. Herewith you are reminded that you never outgrow your need for butterscotch brownies.*

- 4 tablespoons (½ stick) butter, melted, plus softened butter for the pan
- 1 cup packed light brown sugar
- 1 large egg
- ¾ cup sifted all-purpose flour
- 1 teaspoon baking powder
- ½ teaspoon salt
- ½ cup chopped walnuts
- 1 teaspoon vanilla extract

Preheat the oven to 350°F. Butter an 8-inch square baking pan. Combine the melted butter and brown sugar in a large bowl. Cool slightly, then stir in the egg. Sift the flour, baking powder, and salt into a small bowl. Stir into the brown sugar mixture. Stir in the walnuts and vanilla. Spread the batter in the prepared pan. Bake for 20 to 25 minutes, or until only a slight imprint remains when touched lightly with your finger. Cut into squares while still warm. These are best eaten within a few days.

Apple-Walnut Bars
(Yugoslav Nut Pita)

Makes 32 small bars

In my "Ethnic" recipe folder, *there's a small collection of Yugoslav recipes from Helen, a* Cook & Tell *subscriber I lost track of a few years ago. When pictures from the Balkans began to fill our television screens and newspapers, I thought of Helen again and looked up her authentic recipes. They brought good news from Yugoslavia— news as old as time, of women baking delicious things for their families and friends with affection and care. I make this very special sweet with all those dear folks in mind, because they are just like my family and my friends and me.*

Pastry

- 1 cup (2 sticks) unsalted butter, softened, plus more for the pan
- Scant 1¼ cups sugar
- 3 large egg yolks
- 3 tablespoons sour cream
- ½ teaspoon vanilla extract
- 3 cups all-purpose flour
- 4 teaspoons baking powder

Filling

- 2 large egg whites
- 1 pound walnuts, finely ground
- 1 medium apple, peeled, cored, and grated
- ½ cup sugar

P reheat the oven to 325°F. Butter a 9-by-13-inch baking pan.

To make the pastry: Using a wooden spoon, cream the 1 cup butter and 1 cup of the sugar in a large bowl. Stir in the egg yolks, sour cream, and vanilla. Combine the flour, baking powder, and remaining scant ¼ cup sugar in a medium bowl. Stir gradually into the butter mixture. Divide the dough in half. Roll out one portion between two sheets of wax paper to fit the baking pan. Peel off the top layer of wax paper and bravely give the dough a quick flip directly over the pan, so it will fall in, more or less covering the bottom of the pan. Trim and fit the dough where necessary.

To make the filling: Beat the egg whites in a medium bowl until stiff. Fold in the walnuts, apple, and sugar. Spread the filling evenly over the dough in the pan. Roll out the remaining dough between two sheets of wax paper to completely cover the filling. Trim and fit as before. Prick the top crust all over with a fork. Bake for 30 to 35 minutes, or until golden brown, watching carefully. Cool thoroughly before cutting into 32 small bars. The bars keep for one week in an airtight container.

Chapter 10

jimmies morsels chips shot ▲ fudgy-wudgy ▶

DUTCH PROCESS 🥤 COCOA.

ANY FLAVOR as long as it's CHOCOLATE ▶

Chocolate Chitchat

▲ H☉T CHOC. 🍵 Chocolat Chaud-oui!

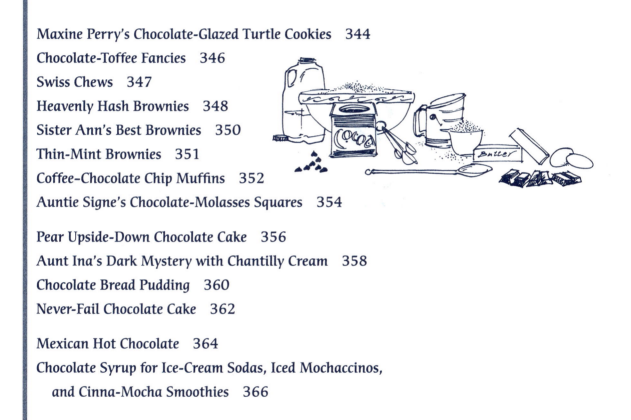

Maxine Perry's Chocolate-Glazed Turtle Cookies

Makes about 3 dozen cookies

These fudgy, brownie-like cookies *from Kathy Petrullo are made in a waffle iron. They're especially fun to make in the summer, when the thought of turning on the oven doesn't turn you on.*

8 tablespoons (1 stick) butter

2 1-ounce squares unsweetened chocolate

³/₄ cup sugar

2 large eggs

1 teaspoon vanilla extract

Pinch of salt

1 cup all-purpose flour

¹/₂ cup chopped almonds or pecans

¹/₄–¹/₂ cup mini semisweet chocolate chips

Chocolate Glaze (recipe follows)

Preheat the waffle iron.

Melt the butter and unsweetened chocolate in a medium saucepan over low heat. Stir in the sugar and remove from the heat. Cool briefly, then whisk in the eggs, vanilla, and salt. Stir in the flour, almonds or pecans, and chocolate chips. Drop by scant tablespoons onto the hot waffle iron, three or four at a time, depending on the size of your waffle iron. Don't try to smooth them out—you want raggedy edges. Immediately close the waffle iron and bake for 45 to 60 seconds. Do not overbake! Make 'em fudgy! Lift off gently with a fork, cool on a rack, and glaze. Store in an airtight container for up to 1 week.

STEP LIVELY TO CATCH UP WITH MAXINE'S TURTLE COOKIES. THEY MOVE FAST!

Chocolate Glaze

6 tablespoons (³/₄ stick) butter
½ cup sugar
3 1-ounce squares unsweetened chocolate
Pinch of salt

1 tablespoon cornstarch
¼ cup milk
¼ cup light cream or half-and-half
1 teaspoon vanilla extract

Put the butter, sugar, chocolate, and a dash of salt in a small saucepan over low heat and stir until melted. Put the cornstarch in a small bowl and stir in the milk, blending well to avoid lumps. Add the cornstarch mixture and the cream or half-and-half to the chocolate mixture. Bring to a boil, stirring constantly until thickened like a pudding. Remove from the heat and stir in the vanilla. Immediately spoon a generous gob of glaze over each cookie, because it sets fairly quickly. In a real hurry? Put a tray of glazed cookies in the fridge for super-quick setting.

Chocolate-Toffee Fancies

Makes 4 dozen cookies

COOK & TELL readers are crazy *about graham crackers and chocolate. Periodically, a recipe for another such delectable thing pops into our mailbox, like this one. These irresistible and utterly easy candylike cookies are perfect to put in lunch boxes or to file in the freezer for a sneaky personal indulgence, one or two at a time.*

12 whole graham crackers, broken at all the perforations into 48 little rectangles
1   cup (2 sticks) butter or margarine
1   cup packed light brown sugar
1   cup chopped pecans
12 ounces (2 cups) semisweet chocolate chips

Preheat the oven to 350°F.

Lay the 48 graham-cracker rectangles cheek by jowl on a 10-by-15-inch jelly-roll pan. It's OK if some bare pan shows around the edges.

Melt the butter in a small saucepan over medium heat. Stir in the brown sugar and bring to a boil. Boil for 3 minutes, stirring constantly. Pour the brown-sugar mixture over the graham crackers and sprinkle the pecans evenly over the top. Bake for 10 minutes, or until the topping is bubbly. Remove from the oven and immediately scatter the chocolate chips over the top. Wait for a second or two until they begin to melt, then spread them like frosting. Cool for at least 10 minutes before cutting or breaking the cookies more or less where the crackers separate, under all that gooey topping.

Swiss Chews

Makes 4 dozen chews

Jane Paull kept this one *a deep, dark-brown secret for a long time, she said, because they're so special. These impressive beauties are a snap to make, if you follow orders and use the kind of cookie sheet called for; I went right out and bought one. The smooth candy-cookie effect and the toasted almonds are what make these goodies so special.*

6	ounces (1 cup) semisweet chocolate chips	¼	teaspoon salt
1	large egg	1	teaspoon vanilla extract
½	cup packed light brown sugar	½	cup slivered almonds, toasted and very finely chopped

Preheat the oven to 325°F.

Melt the chocolate chips in the top of a double boiler over simmering water or in a bowl in the microwave. Beat the egg in a medium bowl. Stir in the brown sugar, salt, and vanilla. Fold in the melted chocolate and almonds. For small chews, drop by half-teaspoons 2 inches apart onto a nonstick cookie sheet. Bake for 9 minutes. It's another one of those "do not overbake" deals, but this time I *really* mean it. Cool on a rack.

Note

Jane says to keep the chews in the freezer in tins, with plastic wrap between layers, because they don't hang around well at room temperature. Kept this way, they're just as good days after baking as when they've just come out of the oven.

Heavenly Hash Brownies

Makes 2 dozen 2-inch brownies

COOK & TELLer Jo McGruder *entered her brownie recipe in a Made-in-a-9-by-13-Inch-Pan recipe contest in the* St. Louis Post-Dispatch *and walked off with a prize in the dessert category. Jo's brownies illustrate a basic* Cook & Tell *dessert tenet: You can never have too much stuff. You've got chopped nuts* and *broken nuts, you've got marshmallows* and *chocolate (not even counting the brownie mix), and you've got frosting. How could you not win with this one? Use all the frosting or pay a fine.*

Brownies

Butter
1 19.8-ounce package brownie mix
1 cup chopped pecans
3 cups mini marshmallows
1 cup coarsely broken pecans

Frosting

8 tablespoons (1 stick) butter
2 1-ounce squares unsweetened chocolate
⅓ cup milk
1 1-pound package confectioners' sugar
1 teaspoon vanilla extract

To make the brownies: Preheat the oven to 350°F. Butter a 9-by-13-inch baking pan.

Make the brownie mix according to the package directions. Stir in the *chopped* pecans. Spoon the batter into the prepared pan. Bake for

25 minutes, or until just set in the center. Remove from the oven. Sprinkle the marshmallows over the hot brownies in the pan. Top with the broken pecans.

To make the frosting: Combine the butter, chocolate, and milk in a medium saucepan over low heat. Cook, stirring often, until the chocolate and butter melt. Remove from the heat. Transfer to a medium bowl and add the confectioners' sugar and vanilla. Using an electric mixer, beat on low speed until smooth. Spread the frosting (don't hold back!) over the hot brownies. Cool in the pan on a rack before cutting.

Sister Ann's Best Brownies

Makes 2 dozen 2-inch brownies

Chief booster, **Bob**, *likes his brownies "good and fudgy." Sisters Susan Quinby and Ann Young step up with their recipe, which produces just the kind he likes, as long as you treat them the way brownies should be treated and don't overbake them.*

²/₃ cup unsalted butter, plus more for the pan	2 teaspoons vanilla extract
1¹/₂ cups sugar	4 large eggs
12 ounces (2 cups) semisweet chocolate chips	1¹/₂ cups all-purpose flour
	¹/₂ teaspoon baking soda
	¹/₂ teaspoon salt

Preheat the oven to 325°F. Butter a 9-by-13-inch baking pan. Combine the ²/₃ cup butter, sugar, and ¹/₄ cup water in a large saucepan and bring to a boil over medium-high heat. Remove from the heat. Stir in the chocolate chips and vanilla until smooth. Transfer to a large bowl and cool thoroughly. Beat in the eggs one at a time. Sift the flour, baking soda, and salt into a medium bowl. Stir into the chocolate mixture just until blended. Pour the batter into the prepared pan. Bake for 35 to 40 minutes, or until just set in the center; do not overbake. Cool in the pan on a rack. Cut into 24 squares.

Thin-Mint Brownies

Makes 16 squares or 32 bars

I've fallen right in step *with the chocolate lobby's current dictum, which advocates upping the chocolate component of every tried-and-true chocolate recipe, and doubled the quantity in the brownie recipe my mother always used. Then I gilded the lily with a frosting that has a softly marbled look.*

8 tablespoons (1 stick) butter, plus more for the pan	2 large eggs
4 1-ounce squares unsweetened chocolate, chopped	½ cup all-purpose flour Pinch of salt
1 cup sugar	16 thin mints (chocolate-covered peppermint patties about the size of a silver dollar)
2 teaspoons vanilla extract	

Preheat the oven to 350°F. Line a 9-inch square pan with foil, leaving a 2-inch overhang for easy lifting out. Butter the foil.

Melt the 8 tablespoons butter and chopped chocolate in a medium saucepan over medium-low heat. Remove from the heat and stir in the sugar and vanilla. Cool for 5 minutes. Beat the eggs in a small bowl. Quickly stir a spoonful of the chocolate mixture into the eggs to temper them, then stir the eggs into the chocolate mixture. Stir in the flour and salt. Spread the batter in the prepared pan. Bake for 25 minutes, or until just set in the center. Put the pan on a rack and immediately distribute the thin mints evenly over the brownies, spreading and swirling them as they begin to melt. Cool thoroughly in the pan. Lift out the entire slab by the foil "handles." Cut on a board into 16 squares or 32 bars.

Coffee-Chocolate Chip Muffins

Makes 6 giant or 12 standard muffins

Gerry Connors sent me his recipe, *"developed from the back of the Bisquick box,"* *which reminded me of a similar one from Jim Schatz. So I knitted them together, adding Jim's coffee, an additional egg, and a whole stick of butter in place of Gerry's wee bit of oil. Now we have muffins! To reheat, zap them in the microwave for maximum gooey-tude.*

8 tablespoons (1 stick) unsalted butter, softened, plus more for the tin

¹/₃ cup sugar

3 tablespoons instant coffee granules

1 teaspoon vanilla extract

²/₃ cups milk

2 large eggs, lightly beaten

2 cups all-purpose baking mix, such as Bisquick

6 ounces (1 cup) semisweet chocolate chips

1 cup chopped walnuts

Preheat the oven to 350°F. Butter a muffin tin or line the cups with paper liners.

Cream the 8 tablespoons butter, sugar, coffee granules, and vanilla in a medium bowl. Combine the milk and eggs in a small bowl. Add the baking mix and milk mixture alternately to the butter mixture, stirring to blend; do not beat or your muffins will be tough. Fold in the chocolate chips and walnuts. Fill the muffin cups nearly full. Bake for

15 to 20 minutes, depending on size, until a tester stuck in the center of a muffin comes out clean. Cool for 10 minutes in the tin on a rack before removing from the tin. Serve warm.

Low-Tech Talk

High tech meets low tech, and they live happily ever after in Sara Tatham's favorite low-tech kitchen gadget: a chopstick.

Less bulky than a wooden spoon, it's the perfect stirrer for melting chocolate in the microwave, because it's wooden and you can leave it in the bowl (but don't use a stick with metallic lettering, to avoid arcing). "If I use a spoon, invariably I set it on the counter," Sara confesses, "and if it comes into contact with a drop of water, awful things happen to the chocolate. I also use a chopstick to clean out the blender after grinding bread or cookie crumbs."

Auntie Signe's Chocolate-Molasses Squares

Makes 32 small squares

COOK & TELL's vote *for Best Alternative Brownie goes to Ruth Hedberg's moist, super-chewy, nut-free, raisin-free, marshmallow-free squares. Almost butterscotchy, but better, they were her Swedish aunt's specialty.*

8 tablespoons (1 stick) butter, plus more for the pans	1 cup all-purpose flour
¼ cup molasses	½ teaspoon baking soda
¾ cup packed light brown sugar	½ teaspoon salt
1 large egg, lightly beaten	12 ounces (2 cups) semisweet chocolate chips

Preheat the oven to 350°F. Butter two 8-inch square pans. Combine the 8 tablespoons butter and molasses in a medium saucepan over medium heat. Add the brown sugar and stir until melted. Cool. Stir in the egg. Sift the flour, baking soda, and salt into a medium bowl. Stir the flour mixture and chocolate chips into the butter mixture. Spread the batter in the prepared pans. It will barely cover the bottoms of the pans, but the baked squares will be just the right thickness, scarcely more than ¼ inch. Bake for 18 to 20 min-

"When my brother and I were growing up, Sunday afternoons were spent with family. Auntie Signe always brought a tin of freshly baked goodies, and we were delighted when it contained her Chocolate-Molasses Squares. I was allowed to have a cup of warm milk mixed with a couple of tablespoons of coffee, which made me feel special. Those were wonderful days."

— Ruth Hedberg

utes, or until the edges have barely begun to shrink from the sides of
the pan. Cool for 5 minutes before cutting into squares.

 **Note**

*Cut the squares into triangles for a fancy presenta-
tion on a tray of sweets.*

Pear Upside-Down Chocolate Cake

Serves 8

And you thought pineapple *was the only fruit that did headstands! Chocolate and pears team up here in a moist, rich, torte-like cake, whose satiny topping echoes the delicate flavor of the fruit.*

Cake

- 3 tablespoons butter
- ½ cup packed light brown sugar
- 8 canned pear halves, drained (reserve the juice)
- 1 1-ounce square unsweetened chocolate, chopped
- ¼ cup vegetable shortening
- 1 cup all-purpose flour
- ⅔ cup granulated sugar
- ½ teaspoon baking soda
- ¼ teaspoon salt
- ⅓ cup milk
- 1 large egg, lightly beaten

Topping

- 1½ tablespoons cornstarch
- 1 cup juice from the drained pears
- 1 teaspoon vanilla extract
- 1 cup heavy cream

To make the cake: Put the butter in a 9-inch round cake pan and place the pan in the oven. Set the oven temperature at 350°F and let the butter melt while the oven preheats; be careful not to burn the butter. Remove from the oven and stir in the brown sugar. Spread the brown-sugar mixture evenly over the bottom of the pan. Arrange the pears cut side down in the bottom of the pan. Set aside.

Melt the chocolate in the top of a double boiler over barely simmering water. Remove from the heat and set aside. Beat the shortening until fluffy in a large bowl. Sift the flour, sugar, baking soda, and salt into a medium bowl. Add to the shortening. Using a pastry blender or two knives, cut the shortening into the flour mixture. Stir in the milk and egg. Add the melted chocolate and beat for 1 minute. Spread the batter over the pears. You'll think there's not enough batter to cover them, but swirl it like thick frosting, pushing it into the valleys between the pears with your spoon. Bake for 45 minutes, or until a tester stuck in the cake comes out clean. Invert onto a platter immediately, with the pears on top. Cool.

To make the topping: Dissolve the cornstarch in the pear juice in a small saucepan over medium-low heat. Cook, stirring constantly, until thickened, about 5 minutes. Remove from the heat and stir in the vanilla. Transfer to a medium bowl and cool to room temperature. Whip the cream until stiff in a medium bowl and fold it in. Spoon the topping over the cake when serving.

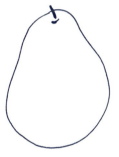

Aunt Ina's Dark Mystery
with Chantilly Cream

Serves 12

An old-fashioned church bazaar *luncheon, staged annu-
ally since 1910, always ends with this cake. Judy Alger received the
recipe from her mother-in-law, who got the recipe from her great-aunt.
It's a low-rise, soft, moist cross between a cake and a steamed pudding
—dark, but with a discreet chocolate flavor. What makes this cake so
scrumptiously rich, but not too? It's a mystery.*

Butter	3 tablespoons all-purpose flour
1 cup chopped dried apricots	3 tablespoons unsweetened
1 tablespoon vanilla extract	cocoa powder
3 large eggs	4 teaspoons baking powder
2 cups chopped pitted dates	1 teaspoon salt
1 cup raisins	
1 cup sugar	Chantilly Cream (recipe
³/₄ cup peeled, cored, and diced	follows)
Granny Smith apple	
(¹/₂ large)	

Preheat the oven to 350°F. Line a 9-by-13-inch baking pan with
parchment paper and butter the paper.

Toss the apricots with the vanilla in a small bowl (see Note).

Lightly beat the eggs in a large bowl. Stir in the apricot mixture,
dates, raisins, sugar, apple, flour, cocoa powder, baking powder, and

salt. Spread the batter in the prepared pan. Bake for 40 minutes, or until set. Cool the cake completely in the pan on a rack. Lift the cake out by the parchment, invert it onto a cookie sheet or cutting board, and peel off the parchment. Cut into serving pieces and serve with Chantilly Cream.

> **Note**
>
> *The original recipe calls for the chopped apricots to soak overnight in 3 tablespoons dark rum.*

Chantilly Cream

1 cup heavy cream
1 teaspoon vanilla extract
$^1/_2$ teaspoon orange extract
   (optional)

$^1/_4$ cup sugar
2 tablespoons sour cream

Chill a medium bowl and the beaters of an electric mixer until very cold.

Combine the cream, vanilla, and orange extract, if using, in the chilled bowl and beat on medium speed for 1 minute. Add the sugar and sour cream and beat on high speed until soft peaks form; do not overbeat. Serve with the cake.

Chocolate Bread Pudding

Serves 4

Don't you love the way *that old favorites eventually come around again, all gussied up with ingredients that cost an arm and a leg, like macaroni and cheese with crème fraîche and the cheese of a thousand syllables? You could get wound up like that with the bread pudding reincarnations now circulating. Or you could pick up a carton of chocolate milk at your local supermarket and put together a bread pudding that's only slightly chic—and* très délicieux *(pardon my French).*

3   tablespoons butter, softened
7   ³/₄-inch-thick slices Italian bread
3   ounces (¹/₂ cup) semisweet chocolate chips

2   cups chocolate milk
3   large eggs
3   tablespoons sugar
    Dash of salt

Preheat the oven to 350°F.
Using 2 tablespoons of the butter, butter the bread slices on one side only. Arrange 3 or 4 of the bread slices standing on edge around the perimeter of a 1-quart soufflé dish, butter side out. Sprinkle a few chocolate chips on the bottom of the dish and layer the remaining bread and chocolate chips into the dish every which way, letting the chips fall where they may and ending with bread, butter side up.

Beat the chocolate milk, eggs, sugar, and salt in a medium bowl and pour over the bread. Press down the bread slices to be sure all the edges get wet, but let them stick out if they float up out of the liquid. Dot with the remaining 1 tablespoon butter. Put the baking dish in a larger roasting pan and pour enough hot water into the roasting pan to come halfway up the sides of the dish. Bake for $1^1/_4$ hours, or until set. Serve warm.

Never-Fail Chocolate Cake

Makes one 9-inch square or round cake

When it's Happy Birthday time *and the cake of their dreams is chocolate, make this one, which Dorothy Frary describes as "moist and rough-textured." She's been baking this cake for all her family birthdays for over thirty years. She found it in the 1957 Hampshire County (Mass.) Extension cookbook.*

8 tablespoons (1 stick) butter, plus more for the pan
1 cup sugar
2 1-ounce squares unsweetened chocolate, chopped
1 cup milk
1 cup all-purpose flour

1 teaspoon baking soda
1 large egg
1 teaspoon vanilla extract

Ice cream
Bittersweet Chocolate Sauce (recipe follows)

Preheat the oven to 350°F. Butter a 9-inch square or round cake pan.

Combine the sugar, chocolate, and milk in a large saucepan and bring to a boil over medium heat. Add the 8 tablespoons butter, remove from the heat, and cool briefly. Beat in the flour, baking soda, egg, and vanilla. Pour the batter into the prepared pan.

> ### 🧤 Note 🧤
>
> *You can double the recipe for a 9-by-13-inch cake. Bake for a few minutes longer, testing for doneness.*

hip! hip! hooray! Happy Birthday! mazel tov!

Bake for 25 to 30 minutes—a wee bit longer for the round pan, because the cake is thicker—or until a tester stuck in the center comes up clean. Remove from the pan and cool on a rack. Frost or top each portion with a scoop of peppermint-stick ice cream, and bathe it all in warm Bittersweet Chocolate Sauce.

Bittersweet Chocolate Sauce

Makes about ¾ cup

This sauce doesn't turn hard *when it hits ice cream.*

2 1-ounce squares unsweetened chocolate	Pinch of salt
½ cup sugar	3 tablespoons butter
	1 teaspoon vanilla extract

"Memorize this recipe for emergencies."

— Rob MacKusick

Melt the chocolate in ¼ cup water in a small saucepan and bring to a boil over medium-high heat, stirring until smooth. Add the sugar and return to a boil. Reduce the heat to medium and simmer, stirring constantly, until thickened and syrupy and the sugar is dissolved, 3 to 4 minutes. Stir in the salt. Remove from the heat and add the butter and vanilla, stirring until thoroughly blended. Serve warm.

Mexican Hot Chocolate

Serves 4 to 6

Technically, you can't call *a cup of cocoa "hot chocolate," because cocoa is made from cocoa powder and hot chocolate from a hunk of chocolate. Fat content figures into it, too. But do we care?*

Make this good hot drink with Mexican overtones and see what people call it when they ask for refills.

2 1-ounce squares unsweetened chocolate	3 cups milk
3 tablespoons sugar	1 heaping teaspoon grated fresh orange zest
½ teaspoon ground cinnamon	¼ teaspoon almond extract
Dash of salt	¼ teaspoon vanilla extract
	Whipped cream, for garnish

Melt the chocolate with 1 cup water in a medium saucepan over low heat, stirring frequently. Meanwhile, combine the sugar, cinnamon, and salt in a small bowl. Gradually stir into the melted chocolate. Bring to a boil over medium heat. Boil for 4 minutes, stirring constantly. Gradually add the milk, stirring constantly. Remove from the heat and stir in the orange zest, almond extract, and vanilla.

Return the pan to low heat and warm gently; do not boil. Using a stick blender or an eggbeater, beat the hot chocolate until frothy. Pour into cups or mugs and garnish with whipped cream.

*I*t's the *sunday-night phone call from my daughter in Phoenix.* I am walking around the house with the phone to my ear, looking for a book from which she needs a reference, and I'm giving my husband, Bob, orders to get the supper tray together.

Mothership to Earth: "We're having popcorn for supper."

Earth to mothership: "Oh," she sighs, remembering the old-time New England Sunday-night menu. "Cheese? Apples?" A pause. Amie is a long way from this Maine island. Then, wistfully: "Cocoa?"

battered
old
popcorn popper

sharp cheese

cocoa
and apples

sunday night
supper

Chocolate Syrup for Ice-Cream Sodas, Iced Mochaccinos, and Cinna-Mocha Smoothies

Makes 2 quarts

This is cool! *It's thinner than Hershey's, and nicer, because it mixes in more easily and because you made it yourself and, therefore, it's practically free, right?*

1 cup unsweetened cocoa powder	1 teaspoon ground cinnamon
	5 cups sugar

Combine the cocoa, cinnamon, and 4 cups warm water in a medium saucepan and bring to a boil over medium-high heat. Gradually stir in the sugar. Remove from the heat as soon as the sugar is dissolved. Store in a covered jar in the fridge for up to 2 weeks.

For 1 Ice-Cream Soda: Pour ⅓ cup chocolate syrup into a tall glass. Add about half as much cream or milk and stir. Add a big scoop of vanilla, chocolate, or coffee ice cream and enough soda water to fill the glass, stirring down the bubbles with a long spoon.

For 1 Iced Mochaccino: Combine ¼ cup chocolate syrup, ¾ cup cold coffee, and ½ cup milk (or more or less of everything) in a blender jar. Cover and whir until light-colored and foamy. Pour into a tall glass.

For 2 Cinna-Mocha Smoothies: Combine ¼ cup chocolate syrup, 1 cup strong, cold coffee, ½ teaspoon ground cinnamon, and 1 frozen banana, cut into chunks, in a blender jar. Cover and whir until thoroughly blended. Pour into two glasses.

"I believe with all my heart, and more so as I get older, that cooking is a real art and a very precious gift we give to others." — Joann Wetmore

To subscribe to Karyl Bannister's *Cook & Tell* newsletter, please send a check ($16) made payable to *Cook & Tell:*

Cook & Tell
Love's Cove
P.O. Box 363
Southport, Maine 04576

Index